The Virginia Beach Harvest Cookbook

Recipes and History
from the Garden Spot of the State

Pleasant Hall in Kempsville, built in 1779, is privately owned. It is one of the few original buildings of the old town of Kempsville still standing. Pen and ink by Janice O. Dool

The Virginia Beach Harvest Cookbook

Recipes and History from the Garden Spot of the State

Mary Reid Barrow

The Donning Company/Publishers
Norfolk/Virginia Beach

With thanks to all the good cooks whose recipes fill this book. Their love of fresh vegetables, seafood, and all the other delicious fruits of this city and, consequently, their enthusiasm for my project are responsible for its very being.

The Donning Company/Publishers
5659 Virginia Beach Boulevard
Norfolk, Virginia 23502

Library of Congress Cataloging in Publication Data

Barrow, Mary Reid
    The Virginia Beach harvest cookbook.

    Includes index.
    1. Cookery, American—Virginia.   2. Virginia Beach (Va.)—Social life and customs.   I. Title.
TX715.B324   1984   641.59755'51   83-16330
ISBN 0-89865-334-7 (pbk.)

Printed in the United States of America

Table of Contents

These recipes are arranged by product rather than by place on the menu for the convenience of those who arrive home from harvesting with a gallon of strawberries, a mess of bluefish, or a bushel of oysters.

Acknowledgments

This book is dedicated to all the fine cooks whose recipes make this book what it is. I first came across many of their recipes in cookbooks published by churches and other organizations in the city. These cookbooks often are very representative of the "flavor" of an area. Most especially I want to thank Etta Mae Land and the Tabernacle Methodist Church cookbooks, *Country Roads,* 1982, and *Table Talk from Tabernacle,* 1974. From the beginning, she understood and appreciated what I was trying to do. I also want to thank Jack Burroughs and *What's Cooking at Charity,* 1962, and Charity United Methodist Church's more recent cookbook, published in 1983; Susan Buchanan and Eastern Shore Chapel Episcopal Church's cookbook, *Holy Chow;* and Anne Callis, Robbin Jordan, and the several editions of *Loaves and Fishes* from Galilee Episcopal Church.

I also am grateful to Beth Murray and the Oceana Officers Wives Club cookbook, *A Flight Plan Before Dinner,* 1982; Janet Werndli and a *Resume of Recipes from Members of the Council of Garden Clubs of Virginia Beach,* 1980; Alice Caffee and the *Virginia Beach Sand Witches Cookbook,* 1978; Susan Woodward, editor of the *Cookbook by Parents, Teachers and Students of Creeds School,* 1981; and Betty Tripp and *Bell Ringers for Old Donation Church,* 1976.

My thanks also go to Judy Humphries who operated a stall at the Virginia Beach Farmer's Market where she sold fresh vegetables raised by her and her husband on their Princess Anne County farm. Other growers who were particularly helpful include Mary Martin of Martin's Strawberry Farm, Mrs. Gordon Oliver of Oliver's Farm Market, Adell Fentress who raises peaches with her husband on Knotts Island, and Mary Williams of Williams Farm.

Virginia Beach Clerk of the Court Curtis Fruit and his staff at Princess Anne Courthouse were supportive as were Dick Cockrell and others at the Virginia Beach Department of Agriculture. The Virginia Department of Agriculture and Consumer Services allowed the use of several of their recipes. I also appreciate the use of recipes from the Virginia Farm Bureau and from the Culinary Arts Program at the Virginia Beach Campus of Tidewater Community College.

Others to whom I am indebted include Lynda Newcomb who typed a good portion of the manuscript; Gray Dodson and Norvell Butler for their wild game recipes; Paula Opheim, former Lynnhaven House administrator, for her enthusiasm and for her recipes; and Mary Jane Borchers, whose husband is director of the Virginia Truck and Ornamentals Research Station, for her recipes. The list goes on and includes Archie Johnson of the Back Bay Wildfowl Guild, Shelby Webster, Willa Engel, and Margaret Allen at the Virginia Beach Campus of Tidewater Community

College, Michelene Mower, and Page Davis. I owe a special thanks to Betty Michelson, a Virginia Beach lawyer, who shared her old Princess Anne County family recipes and letters with me.

As always, the staff at Information Services in the Virginia Beach Public Library and at the Sargeant Memorial Room in the Norfolk Public Library were most helpful.

My appreciation also goes to Dennis Hartig, Virginia Beach editor of *The Virginian-Pilot* and *The Ledger-Star.* Much of the historical material in this book appeared in my column, "History Beat," in the *Beacon,* the local insert in the *Pilot* and *Ledger.*

I want to thank *Bon Appetit* for the use of two of Peter Coe's recipes which originally appeared in the May 1983 issue and *Audubon Magazine* for the use of Ruth Ohlmeyer's persimmon recipes. I also appreciate the use of quotes from the *Naval Campaigns of Count de Grasse* by Karl Gustaf Tornquist, translated by Amandus Johnson, published by the Swedish Colonial Society, 1942; *Beat the Last Drum* by Thomas F. Fleming, St. Martin's Press, Inc., 1963, and *I Wouldn't Take Nothing for My Journey, Two Centuries of An Afro-American Minister's Family* by Dr. Leonidas C. Berry, Johnson Publishing Co., 1982.

The artwork comes from various sources. Most helpful was Janice O. Dool who graciously consented to the use of her pen and ink sketches of historical sites in Virginia Beach. These have been for sale over the years to the public as prints and as note paper. Mary Lynn Perney lent her enthusiasm and her pen and watercolor of Munden's Store. "Canada Geese" is the work of artist Jan Southard and it won the Back Bay Wildfowl Guild contest for art work to be used as a free print give-away at the 1983 Mid-Atlantic Wildfowl Guild Show. Alice Walter for the Francis Land house; Bill Miller, owner of the Duck-In for Rick Fusco's illustration of the Duck-In, and Chris Nicholson, an art student at the Virginia Beach Campus of Tidewater College, for his illustration of Mercer's Boathouse.

The Virginia Beach Maritime Historical Museum has allowed the use of drawings by Charles Sibley, Emily Whaley, Polly Blackford, and the late A. B. Jackson. These once were part of a history exhibit at the Virginia Beach Arts Center and now belong to the Maritime Historical Museum and are available for sale in postcard form at the museum.

The Virginia Beach Bank of Commerce was kind enough to allow the use of several sketches of places of local interest which they have given to their customers over the years.

I also want to thank Robie Ray, photographer at *The Virginian-Pilot* and *The Ledger-Star,* for the use of his photograph of me.

Princess Anne County:
The Garden Spot of the State

An Introduction

On that day in 1607 at Cape Henry when the first colonists discovered the "beautiful strawberries" and the large oysters, "delicate in taste," they were introduced to the land of plenty this area would become.

The Indians had been enjoying the fruits of the land and sea long before the settlers arrived. For the first 200 years, the settlers were content to follow in the Indians' footsteps, raising corn and other grains, simple kitchen gardens, and tobacco, as the cash crop.

Princess Anne County soil, however, wasn't well suited to tobacco, and the area never thrived like those further inland, which became rich off the weed. With the advent of the agricultural revolution in the South and the coming of the steamboat and railroad, Princess Anne County came into its own.

The county held its first Agricultural Fair in the little town of Kempsville in 1852, preceding the first Virginia State Fair by a full year. Sponsored by the Princess Anne County Agricultural Society, the two-day event was an exhibit of prize livestock and vegetables.

The *Norfolk Argus* reported that the fair "far exceeded public expectations.... It proves that the farmers in this section have the spirit and the means to present as good a fair as any in the land."

"The county of Princess Anne is destined in a few years to become the garden spot of the state," another report said. "Independent of its proximity to navigation and its inexhaustible piscatorial resources, it contains to the extent of its territory a larger valuable and productive land than any other county in Virginia...."

By the turn of the century, 1,423 farms in Princess Anne County, along with commercial oystermen and hunters, were supplying vegetables, hogs, Princess Anne turkeys, cartloads of wild game, and barrels of oysters to be shipped to busy northern cities and to the luxurious resort town of Virginia Beach.

Even after the merger of Princess Anne County and Virginia Beach in 1963, the city was known for its agriculture. "The largest resort city in the world" also was among the top one hundred counties in the nation in the production of strawberries, sweet potatoes, and snap beans.

Today the story is changing. As another of the city's top industries, the homebuilding industry, continues to grow, agricultural production has

3

begun to dwindle. Because pick-your-own operations are now the most profitable way to grow vegetables in an area as populated as this is, Virginia Beach residents don't notice the decline in farming, however.

Instead, local residents have a wealth of produce from the land at their very doorstep. With a little extra effort, they still can find "beautiful strawberries" and large oysters, "delicate in taste" within their own city limits.

Blackbeard the pirate marauded the Virginia coast in the early 1700s. Drawing by A. B. Jackson. Courtesy of the Virginia Beach Maritime Historical Museum

Fruit and Nuts

*Kempsville Courthouse, built around 1783, was the fourth of five
courthouses in Princess Anne County and has been destroyed to make way
for development. Pen and ink by Janice O. Dool*

Very Fertile Country

Karl Gustaf Tornquist was a Swede who served with the French Navy during the Revolutionary War. He kept a diary and wrote the following about the land around the Chesapeake Bay.

The country is very fertile, an average crop-yield gives sufficient sustenance for its owner the next year. Except for this advantage these inhabitants could never have withstood a 6 years' war; for although 12,000 acres in the neighborhood have been fallow each year for lack of farmers, who at the age of 15 were sent to camp; yet now during a severe siege they had sufficient provisions to supply an army of 15,000 men and a fleet of 45 sails, in spite of all the ravages a bitter enemy had perpetrated during his march through the country.

The products of the country are, beside quantities of tobacco, also Indian wheat (maize), excellent medicinal herbs and fruit in abundance. They make the best cider of apples, [and] their brandy from peaches; of the latter fruit they have unusual quantities. The rivers abound in fish, and the primeval forests, consisting of numerous large and hard tree varieties, together with oak, birch, fir and spruce, are rich in game.

—From *The Naval Campaigns of Count de Grasse*
by Karl Gustaf Tornquist
translated by Amandus Johnson, 1942

Hot Apple Cider

The Holland Produce Company makes fresh pressed apple cider daily at the Virginia Beach Farmer's Market. For a hot party drink on a cool fall evening, they suggest adding cinnamon sticks, cloves, and lemon slices to the basket of a party-size automatic coffee pot. Perk a half gallon of cider through the pot. Not only will the cider taste spicey but your house will smell good, too.

—Holland Produce Company

Hot Cider Punch

This punch is served at the Colonial Dinner, a fall harvest feast, at Tabernacle United Methodist Church.

Yield: 5 quarts

2 cups water
1 tablespoon ground ginger
1 tablespoon ground nutmeg
6 to 10 whole cloves
6 to 10 whole allspice
3 or 4 sticks (2 inches) cinnamon
1 gallon apple cider
1½ cups sugar
1½ cups light brown sugar, firmly packed
1½ cups dark brown sugar, firmly packed
1 large orange, sliced, then each slice quartered

Combine water and spices in a large saucepan; cover and bring to a boil. Boil 10 minutes. Add cider and sugars and mix. Simmer for 10 minutes more. Stir frequently. Stir in orange slices the last five minutes. Serve warm.

—Etta Mae Land
Country Roads Cookbook
Tabernacle United Methodist Church, 1981

Chutney

Jane Tucker serves her homemade chutney, along with ground peanuts and shredded coconut, as an accompaniment to curried shrimp. She says chutney can be made with firm and slightly underripe apples or pears.

Yield: 5 to 6 pints

1 lemon, seeds removed
   and chopped
1 garlic clove, skinned,
   peeled, and chopped
5 cups peeled, chopped
   apples or pears
1½ cups seedless raisins
2¼ cups brown sugar
¾ cup chopped crystalized
   ginger
1½ teaspoons salt
¼ teaspoon cayenne pepper
2 cups cider vinegar

Simmer all ingredients until fruit is tender. Pack in sterilized jars and seal.

—Jane Tucker

Fresh Apple Cake

Yield: 1 tube cake

1⅓ cup vegetable oil
3 eggs
2 teaspoons vanilla extract
2¾ cups flour
1 teaspoon baking soda
1 teaspoon baking soda
2 teaspoons ground
   cinnamon
½ teaspoon salt
4 cups fresh chopped
   apples
½ cup raisins
½ cup chopped nuts

Preheat oven to 350 degrees F. Mix oil, eggs, sugar, and vanilla. Sift and add flour, soda, cinnamon, and salt. Mix in apples, raisins, and nuts. Batter will be rather stiff. Bake in a greased and floured tube pan for 40 minutes. Then reduce heat to 325 degrees F. for about 30 minutes more, or until done.

Note: Raisins don't sink to the bottom if you mince them.

Amounts of raisins and nuts may be changed to suit your preference.

—Shelby Webster

The Adam Thoroughgood House, built in the mid-1600s, is one of the oldest brick houses in America. It is in Virginia Beach, but owned by the city of Norfolk. Pen and ink by Janice O. Dool

Whole Apple Dumplings

This is an old family recipe belonging to Alice Pfingst, manager of the Adam Thoroughgood House. Adam Thoroughgood was one of the first settlers in Virginia Beach. The house, built in the mid-1600s, probably by the original Adam's son, is one of the oldest brick houses still standing in the United States. Located in the Thoroughgood section of Virginia Beach, the house is owned and maintained by the city of Norfolk.

Yield: 6 servings

Pie dough for a two-crust
   pie
6 apples, peeled and cored
Sugar, butter, and ground
   cinnamon as needed

Syrup
¼ cup (½ stick) butter
1 cup sugar
1 cup water
1 teaspoon ground
   cinnamon

Preheat oven to 350 degrees F. Roll out dough and cut into six squares large enough to cover apples. Place an apple in center of square of dough. Sprinkle sugar and cinnamon and add a dot of butter to the core of each apple. Wrap apple securely in dough and pinch top closed. Repeat with remainder of apples. Place in pan and bake for 20 minutes until dough begins to set. In the meantime, heat syrup ingredients on stove until butter is melted and sugar is dissolved. After 20 minutes, begin to baste dumplings with syrup, continuing to baste occasionally until done, about 30 more minutes.

—Alice Pfingst, Manager
Adam Thoroughgood House

11

Apple Dumplings

Yield: 12 dumplings

2 cups sugar
2 cups water
¼ teaspoon ground
   cinnamon
¼ teaspoon nutmeg
¼ cup (½ stick) butter
6 apples
2 cups flour
1 teaspoon salt
2 teaspoons baking powder
¾ cup vegetable shortening
½ cup milk
Sugar, cinnamon, nutmeg,
   and butter as needed

Preheat oven to 450 degrees F. Make syrup of sugar, water, spices, and butter. Pare and core apples; cut in eighths. Sift flour, salt, and baking powder; cut in shortening. Add milk, all at once, and stir until dough follows fork around bowl. Roll ¼ inch thick on lightly floured board; cut in 5-inch squares. Arrange four pieces of apple on each square; sprinkle generously with sugar, cinnamon, and nutmeg. Dot with butter, fold corners to center, and pinch edges together. Place in greased baking pan one inch apart. Pour over syrup. Can be made in one large roll, pulled together loosely. Any fruit may be used (cherry, peach, blackberry, etc.) Bake 25 to 30 minutes or until dumplings are done.

—Alice Hancock
What's Cooking at Charity
Charity United Methodist Church, 1982

Banana Wheat Quick Bread

Yield: 1 9-by-5-inch loaf

1¼ cups flour
½ cup whole wheat flour
1 cup sugar
1 teaspoon salt
1 teaspoon baking soda
3 large thinly-sliced ripe
   bananas
¼ cup butter or margarine,
   at room temperature
2 tablespoons orange or
   lemon juice
1 egg
½ cup raisins
½ cup chopped nuts

Preheat oven to 325 degrees F. Combine all ingredients except raisins and nuts in a large mixer bowl. Blend at low speed and then beat 3 minutes at medium speed. Fold in raisins and nuts. Pour into greased and floured 9-by-5-inch loaf pan. Bake for 60 to 70 minutes until inserted toothpick comes out clean. Remove from pan. Cool. Wrap in foil. Bread will mellow with storage.

—Willa Engel

Banana Luncheon Bread

Yield: 1 loaf

2 cups flour
1 teaspoon baking powder
1 teaspoon salt
½ teaspoon baking soda
1 cup sugar
½ cup vegetable shortening
2 eggs
1 cup mashed ripe bananas
½ cup chopped pecans or
  walnuts

Preheat oven to 350 degrees F. Sift flour, baking powder, salt, soda, and sugar into bowl. Add shortening, eggs, and bananas. Beat 2½ minutes with electric mixer. Add nuts. Bake in greased loaf pan 60 to 70 minutes.

—Margene Sullivan

Blueberry Custard Pie

The Virginia Beach Truck and Ornamentals Research Station, an independent state agency, is located in Virginia Beach. Their experiments raising fruits, vegetables, and ornamental plants has enhanced the quality of local produce and nursery plants for about fifty years. They hope to introduce "pick-your-own" blueberries to the Tidewater area. The director of the station, Dr. Ed Borchers, often experiments with the plants in his own garden before they are grown at the station, as he did with blueberries. His wife Mary Jane enjoys cooking the fruits of his labor. This blueberry pie is an old family recipe of hers.

Yield: 1 9-inch pie

1 quart blueberries, washed
  and well-drained
1 9-inch pie shell, unbaked
⅔ or ¾ cup sugar,
  depending on sweetness
  of fruit
3 tablespoons flour
2 large or 3 small eggs
1¼ cups milk

Preheat oven to 425 degrees F. Add blueberries to pie shell. In a blender, blend until smooth the sugar, flour, eggs, and milk. Pour over berries. Bake for 25 to 30 minutes until custard is barely set.

Note: This pie can also be made with strawberries, but ¼ cup of cornstarch should be substituted for the flour.

—Mary Jane Borchers

Coconut Pie

In the spring of 1886, the bark *May Queen* went aground near Little Island Life Saving Station and lost her whole cargo of 300,000 coconuts to the sea. Soon coconuts were strewn along the beach for several miles. People walking along the beach would drink the milk and toss the shells aside. For several years thereafter coconuts continued to mark the high tide line. Today the closest anyone on the beach comes to coconuts is coconut-scented suntan lotion. Off the beach, Virginia Allen's pie makes good use of a fresh coconut.

Yield: 1 pie

2 eggs
1 cup sugar
1½ cups evaporated milk, undiluted
2 cups freshly grated coconut
1 teaspoon vanilla extract
Dash salt
1 9-inch pie shell, unbaked

Preheat oven to 425 degrees F. Beat eggs, add sugar, stir in remaining ingredients in order given. Pour into unbaked pie shell and bake 10 minutes. Reduce heat to 350 degrees F. and bake 30 minutes longer, or until firm.

—Virginia Allen

Artist's depiction of the old town of Kempe's Landing in the 1700s. Drawing by Emily Whaley. Courtesy of the Virginia Beach Maritime Historical Museum

Fig Cake

Mrs. Oliver uses this cake as a holiday gift and mixes up several batches of the dry ingredients, storing them in plastic bags ready to mix with the wet ingredients.

Yield: 1 10-inch tube cake

1½ cups sugar
2¼ cups cake flour
1 teaspoon baking soda
1 teaspoon salt
1 teaspoon ground nutmeg
1 teaspoon ground cinnamon
½ teaspoon ground allspice
½ teaspoon ground cloves
1 cup vegetable oil
3 eggs
1 cup buttermilk
1 tablespoon vanilla extract
1 full cup fig preserves, chopped
½ cup nuts, chopped

Buttermilk Glaze
¼ cup buttermilk
½ cup sugar
¼ teaspoon baking soda
1½ teaspoons cornstarch
¼ cup butter or margarine
½ teaspoon vanilla extract

Preheat oven to 350 degrees F. Combine dry ingredients in bowl. Add oil, beating well. Add eggs, beating well. Add buttermilk and vanilla, mixing well. Stir in preserves and pecans. Pour into greased and floured 10-inch tube pan or bundt pan. Bake 1 hour and 15 minutes. Cool 10 minutes. Remove from pan and pour warm buttermilk glaze over warm cake and store in refrigerator. To make glaze, combine first five ingredients in saucepan. Bring to a boil. Cool slightly. Stir in vanilla. Cool a little more and pour all over cake.

—Oliver's Farm Market
Mrs. Gordon Oliver

Fig Preserves

This recipe belonged to Betty Barco's grandmother. She suggests working with no more than five pounds of figs at a time. She likes hers to taste "lemony" but says the amount of lemons can be adjusted to taste. The rule of thumb is three-fourths of a pound of sugar to every pound of figs.

Yield: about 10 pints

5 pounds figs, quartered
3 lemons, sliced very thin
   and seeds removed
3¾ pounds sugar

Combine figs and lemons. Pour sugar over all; do not stir. Allow to sit overnight. The next morning cook fig mixture over very low heat, stirring occasionally, until transparent and very thick, approximately 2 hours. Pour into hot, sterilized jars and seal immediately.

—Betty Barco

Grape Pie

Many farmers have their own grapevines. Betty Michelson's great-grandmother enjoyed this pie at "Woodland" in the area where Baycliff is now.

Yield: 1 9-inch pie

5 cups Concord grapes
1 cup sugar
2 tablespoons cornstarch
½ teaspoon salt
1 tablespoon lemon juice
1 9-inch pie crust, unbaked
Dough for lattice top

Pull the grapes from the stems. Slip off the skins and keep them separate from the pulp. Heat the juice and pulp for about 5 minutes. Then run through a sieve to remove the seeds. Combine sugar, cornstarch, and salt with the pulp and cook about 10 minutes stirring constantly. Add grape skins and lemon juice and pour into pastry shell. Preheat oven to 375 degrees F. Cover top with a lattice of crust and bake for 30 minutes or until set.

—Betty Michelson

Scuppernong Wine

This recipe belonged to Katie Miller's grandmother who served it every evening for dinner. Even today, tradition dictates that Mrs. Miller buy grape wine for special occasions.

Yield: 12 gallons

10 gallons scuppernong
  grapes, washed
10 pounds sugar
Corn whiskey as needed

Place grapes and sugar in a keg. Cover with boiling water and set aside for five days. Mash grapes to a pulp. Strain through a double cheesecloth bag, sweetening to taste. Place mixture back in keg and skim off foam every two days, adding sugar if mixture is too tart. After ten days, pour off clear wine. Continue pouring off clear wine each day until there is no muddy wine at the bottom. At the end of thirty days "to make a kick," put 1 pint of pure corn whiskey or brandy to 1 gallon of wine and place in rubber half-gallon jars with rubber seals. The longer it stands, the stronger it gets. Do not use any vessel that has had vinegar in it.

—Katie Miller

Gertie's Lemon Nut Bread

Yield: 2 loaves

2 cups sugar
1 cup (2 sticks) butter,
   at room temperature
4 eggs, separated
3½ cups flour
1 teaspoon salt
2 tablespoons baking
   powder
1¼ cups milk
1 cup chopped pecans
Grated rind and juice of
   2 lemons
½ cup confectioner's sugar

Preheat oven to 350 degrees F. Cream sugar and butter. Add egg yolks and beat well. Mix dry ingredients and add alternately with milk to sugar and butter mixture. Add nuts and rind. Beat egg whites until soft peaks form. Fold into mixture. Pour into two greased 9-by-5-inch loaf pans and bake for 55 minutes. Mix lemon juice and confectioner's sugar and pour over loaves while still hot. Leave in pans 1 hour before removing.

—Willa Engel

Lemon Chess Pie

This is a favorite at Tabernacle United Methodist Church's annual Colonial Dinner.

Yield: 1 pie

1⅔ cups sugar
1 tablespoon flour
1 tablespoon cornmeal
4 eggs, unbeaten
4 tablespoons melted butter
   (no margarine)
4 tablespoons milk
4 tablespoons lemon juice
   (fresh is best)
Grated rind of 1 lemon
1 9-inch pastry shell,
   unbaked

Preheat oven to 375 degrees F. Combine sugar, flour, and cornmeal; mix lightly with fork. Add next five ingredients and beat until smooth. Pour into unbaked pie shell. Bake about 35 minutes or until top is golden brown. Serve warm.

—Alta Walters
Country Roads Cookbook
Tabernacle United Methodist Church, 1981

Lemon Pound Cake

Yield: 1 10-inch tube cake

1 cup (2 sticks) butter or
    margarine, at room
    temperature
3 cups sugar
½ cup shortening
6 eggs
3 cups flour
½ teaspoon baking powder
½ teaspoon salt
1 teaspoon vanilla extract
2 teaspoons lemon extract
1 cup milk

Preheat oven to 325 degrees F. Cream butter, shortening, and sugar. Add eggs one at a time, mixing well after each addition. Sift together flour, baking powder, and salt. Add dry ingredients alternately with the milk and flavorings, beginning and ending with the flour mixture. Bake in a well-greased and floured 10-inch tube pan for 1 hour and 20 minutes.

—Mrs. B. Noel Fallwell

Lemon Supreme Special Cake

Yield: 1 10-inch tube cake

1 10-ounce lemon cake mix
½ cup sugar
¾ cup vegetable oil
1 cup apricot nectar
4 eggs

Glaze
1 cup confectioner's sugar
Juice of 1 lemon

Preheat oven to 325 degrees F. Mix cake mix, sugar, oil, and nectar together. Next add 1 egg at a time. Bake in tube pan for 1 hour. Cool right side up for 15 minutes; remove from pan. Blend sugar and lemon juice together. Pour mixed glaze over cake while still warm.

—Nita Grimstead

Mrs. Smith's Cold Lemon Soufflé

Yield: 6 servings

½ cup sugar
1 envelope (tablespoon) gelatin
¼ teaspoon salt
1 cup water
3 eggs, separated
1 tablespoon grated lemon rind
3 to 4 tablespoons lemon juice
⅓ cup sugar
1 cup heavy cream, whipped

In medium saucepan combine ½ cup sugar with gelatin and salt. Stir in water. Beat egg yolks and add to sugar mixture. Cook over medium heat stirring constantly until mixture begins to bubble and is slightly thickened. Cool. Stir in lemon juice and rind. Beat egg whites until frothy. Gradually add ⅓ cup sugar and beat until mixture holds its peak. Fold into gelatin along with whipped cream. Refrigerate at least 4 hours before serving.

—Isabel Dunn

Melons: A Tory's Downfall

Princess Anne County harbored quite a number of Tories during the Revolutionary War. In their eagerness to court the British with their fine county produce, one group of Tories unwittingly gave their hand away to the French Navy. According to Thomas J. Fleming in *Beat the Last Drum,* a book about the siege of Yorktown, a number of small boats left shore only hours after Admiral de Grasse's French fleet dropped anchor in the Bay. A man identified as "one of the principal citizens of Virginia," along with others, went up to one of the ships and asked for the flagship of Lord Rodney, the admiral in charge of the British West Indies Fleet. A French sailor who could speak English well asked the whole group aboard and took them to the ship's captain who informed them they were prisoners. In the boat were "excellent melons and many other refreshments which the delighted officers promptly ate, with frequent toasts to Lord Rodney."

—St. Martin's Press Inc.
Copyright © 1963 by Thomas J. Fleming

Melon and Prosciutto Soup

Michelene Mower suggests substituting zucchini or cucumbers and smoked ham and chives. "Experiment," she says.

Yield: 6 servings

2 cups yogurt
1 cup soda water
½ cup heavy cream
1 cup *each* julienne strips of
   melon and prosciutto
⅓ cup chopped fresh mint
Salt and pepper

Combine all ingredients and chill. Serves six.

          —Michelene Mower

Cantaloupe Hints

Add seedless grapes and slivered almonds to your favorite chicken salad recipe. Prepare one-half cantaloupe per person and mound chicken salad in cavity.

    Add a scoop of vanilla ice cream to the cavity of one-half a cantaloupe or use small melon balls as a topping for vanilla ice cream.

          —Dorcas Boudreau
          Bayville Farm

Knotts Island Peaches

Growing peaches in Tidewater takes a lot of hard work because of the danger of frost and the abundance of pests due to the humidity. Knotts Island, however, with its sandy soil is surrounded by so much water that the chance of frost is lessened. The area is much more suitable for peaches than the rest of Virginia Beach. A "micro-climate," horticulturists call it.

Growers there cultivate a variety of peaches which ripen from late June to late August. Knotts Island peaches, as they are fondly known, can be found at some markets, roadside stands, and the Farmer's Market. Many of the growers also run pick-your-own operations at their orchards.

Great-Aunt Jennie's Brandy Peaches

Weigh peaches and to every pound allow ¾ pound sugar. Make syrup by adding 1 pint of water to every 3 pounds of sugar. Add cinnamon and cloves to taste. Place peaches in syrup and cook until you can stick a straw in them. As they soften take out and lay on plate. Boil syrup until quite thick. Cool. Place peaches in jars and pour equal parts syrup and brandy over them.

—Ruth Barrow

Great-Aunt Jennie's Pickled Peaches

Weigh peaches and to every 3 pounds, allow 1 pound of sugar and ½ cup vinegar. Scald this mixture each morning for six mornings and pour over fruit in a stone crock. On the seventh day, add cloves and mace to taste and fruit to syrup and simmer until peaches are tender (10 minutes). Pack peaches and syrup in jars and add a little fresh vinegar and sugar to each jar.

—Ruth Barrow

Summertime Fresh Fruit Salad

Yield: 3 servings

3 peaches
Lemon juice as needed
3 handfuls of blueberries
16 white grapes, halved
3 teaspoons honey

Peel and slice peaches; sprinkle slices with lemon juice. When ready to serve, mix fruit with honey.

—Hannah Moore

Peach Cobbler

Bill and Adell Fentress had the first peach orchards on Knotts Island, and they raise enough varieties to keep them in peaches right on through the summer.

Yield: 6 servings

2 cups sliced fresh peaches
1½ cups sugar, divided
¾ cup flour
2 teaspoons baking powder
½ teaspoon salt
¾ cup milk
½ cup (1 stick) butter or
    margarine

Preheat oven to 350 degrees F. Sprinkle peaches with ¾ cup sugar and set aside to absorb sugar. Sift flour, sugar, baking powder, and salt together. Add milk and mix. Melt butter in a 1½-quart casserole. Pour batter over top margarine. Add peaches, speading evenly over batter. Bake 35 minutes or until batter (which will rise up to cover peaches) is golden brown.

—Adell Fentress

Super-Simple Knotts Island Peach Ice Cream

Yield: 1½ quarts ice cream

1 quart ripe peaches
Sugar to taste
2 cans evaporated milk

Peel peaches and cut into medium to small pieces. Sweeten with sugar to taste. Freeze the milk until half frozen; then put milk in mixer and beat well until light and fluffy. Pour in peaches and partially freeze. Take out of freezer and beat again to make it fine and light. Freeze until hard.

—Lois Waterfield

Peach Dumplings

Yield: 6 servings

Filling
6 tablespoons sugar
½ teaspoon ground nutmeg
½ teaspoon ground cinnamon
2 tablespoons butter

Syrup
1 cup water
¾ cup sugar
¼ teaspoon ground cinnamon
½ teaspoon ground nutmeg
3 tablespoons butter

Double recipe of 9″ pie crust, rolled thin
6 freestone peaches, halved and pitted

To make filling: mix sugar, nutmeg, and cinnamon. Cut butter into mixture.

To make syrup: combine water, sugar, cinnamon, nutmeg, and butter in a pan. Bring to a boil. Set aside. Preheat oven to 325 degrees F. Cut pie crust into squares large enough to wrap one whole peach. Place half the peach on the crust and fill cavity with tablespoon of filling. Place other half of peach on top. Fold crust over top of peach and seal. Repeat with other five peaches. Place dumplings into deep baking dish and pour syrup over them. Bake about 35 minutes or until crust is brown and peaches are tender.

—Aretha Lane

Peanut Soup

Yield: 6 servings

8 ounces roasted peanuts,
  ground into paste (or
  1 cup peanut butter)
2 cups milk
1 onion, minced
2 tablespoons butter
2 tablespoons flour
2 cups beef consommé
6 ounces port, sherry, or
  brandy

Simmer peanut paste with milk and onion for about 1 hour. Melt butter and add flour, stirring until lumps are gone. Add consommé and cook until thickened. Add the peanut mixture to the consommé and strain if using ground nuts. Add port, sherry, or brandy, and serve piping hot.

—Jane Tucker

Peanut Biscuits

Yield: 1 dozen

2 tablespoons peanut butter
⅔ cup milk
2 cups packaged baking
  mix
Melted butter as needed
Chopped unsalted peanuts

In blender whirl together peanut butter and milk; blend into baking mix according to directions on package. Roll dough out; cut into biscuits, brush with melted butter, and sprinkle with chopped nuts. Arrange on baking sheet and bake according to directions on baking mix package.

—From "Made in Virginia" luncheon
by Culinary Arts students at the
Virginia Beach Campus of
Tidewater Community College

Peanut Bread

Yield: 1 loaf

1¾ cups flour
1 teaspoon baking soda
½ teaspoon salt
1 cup brown sugar, packed
⅓ cup peanut butter
1 egg, well-beaten
1 cup buttermilk
1 cup crushed peanuts

Preheat oven to 350 degrees F. Sift flour; measure and resift three times with soda and salt. Blend sugar into peanut butter. Stir in well-beaten egg and beat until smooth. Add flour mixture and buttermilk alternately, beating until smooth after each addition; add crushed peanuts. Turn into greased loaf pan. Bake in moderate oven for 1 hour until brown.

—Virginia Farm Bureau

Jumbo Oatmeal Peanut Butter Cookies

Yield: 3 dozen 3-inch cookies

¾ cup butter or margarine,
    at room temperature
½ cup peanut butter
1 cup sugar
1 cup brown sugar, firmly
    packed
2 eggs
¼ cup milk
1 teaspoon vanilla extract
2 cups sifted flour
1 teaspoon baking soda
1 teaspoon salt
1 teaspoon ground
    cinnamon
1½ cups quick-cooking oats
1 cup raisins

Preheat oven to 350 degrees F. Cream together first four ingredients until smooth and creamy. Add eggs, milk, and vanilla; blend well. Sift together flour, baking soda, salt, and cinnamon; stir into creamed mixture. Blend in oats and raisins. Drop by tablespoonfuls onto greased baking sheets about two inches apart. Bake for 15 minutes or until done.

—Virginia Farm Bureau

Janie's Peanut Butter Ice Cream Pie

Yield: 1 9-inch pie

Oreo Crust
24 Oreo cookies, crushed
¼ cup (½ stick) butter

Peanut Butter Filling
4 egg whites
½ cup honey
1 quart vanilla ice cream,
    softened
1 cup peanut butter (fresh
    ground)
1 cup heavy cream,
    whipped

Blend Oreo cookie crumbs and butter. Line pie pan with crumb mixture. Beat egg whites and honey in double boiler making marshmallow. Blend ice cream and peanut butter and fold into marshmallow. Fold in whipped cream. Pour into Oreo crust and freeze.

—Page Davis

Sugar-Coated Peanuts

Yield: 2 cups

1 cup sugar
½ cup water
2 cups raw shelled peanuts,
    skins on

Preheat oven to 300 degrees F. Dissolve sugar in water in saucepan over medium heat. Add peanuts and continue to cook over medium heat, stirring frequently. Cook until peanuts are completely sugared (coated and no syrup left). Pour and spread over ungreased cookie sheet and bake for 30 minutes, stirring at five-minute intervals with a metal spatula. Recipe is easily doubled.

—Virginia Beach Farm Bureau

Gertie's Pecan Pie

Yield: 1 9-inch pie

3 eggs, lightly beaten
1 cup sugar
1 cup dark corn syrup
2 tablespoons melted butter
1 teaspoon vanilla extract
Pinch salt
1 cup pecans
1 9-inch pie shell, unbaked

Preheat oven to 425 degrees F. Mix first six ingredients well. Add pecans. Pour into pie shell and bake for 10 minutes. Reduce heat to 325 degrees F. and continue baking until filling is set, about 55 minutes.

—Willa Engel

Strawberries

Strawberries are here in May and gone in June, and few people would regard them as having any lasting impact. Instant gustatory gratification is the strawberry's claim to fame, except in Virginia Beach.

Here, the staying power of the berry is immortalized forever by a wreath of strawberry leaves encircling the Virginia Beach city seal. The story began in 1607 when Christopher Newport and his band of settlers were exploring the land beyond Cape Henry. The sight of wild strawberries was enough to distract them from more serious pursuits.

"Beautiful strawberries, four times bigger and better than ours in England," they extolled.

We can thank those "beautiful strawberries" for every modern variety of strawberry we eat today, say the botanists. *Fragaria virginiana* was carried back to Europe and was crossed with European strawberries long before the end of the 1600s.

Commercial production of strawberries in the United States began in the 1880s. By 1855, they were commercially cultivated in Virginia Beach and by the turn of the century the city was a leader in strawberry production in the nation. The berries were shipped, both frozen and fresh, to the large northern cities.

Today, however, the high cost of labor has made it prohibitive for the farmer to pick and process his own berries. Today all the Virginia Beach farmers have "pick-your-own" operations. What is grown here stays here. The Virginia Beach strawberry has come full circle.

How to Pick Strawberries

To pick strawberries, always break the stem by pinching between the thumb and forefinger. Do not remove caps or wash berries until you are ready to use them. Removal of the cap allows moisture in berries to escape. Refrigerate berries and use within two to three days.

—Virginia Department of Agriculture
and Consumer Services

How to Freeze Individual Whole Berries

Wash berries, but do not remove caps. Dry berries, place on cookie sheet, and place in freezer. When frozen, pack berries in freezer bag or container.

When ready to serve, pour out amount needed; return remainder immediately to freezer. Allow to thaw slightly, remove caps, and prepare for serving.

—Virginia Department of Agriculture
and Consumer Services

How to Freeze Strawberries with Sugar or Syrup

To prepare for freezing, sort, wash with cap on in cold water, drain, and remove caps.

Whole or Crushed Berries with Sugar
In a shallow pan, add ¾ cup sugar to each quart of berries and mix thoroughly. Pack, leaving ½ inch headroom. Seal; freeze.

Whole Berries with Syrup
Cover berries with cold 50-percent syrup. Leave appropriate headroom. Seal; freeze.

A 50-percent syrup is made by dissolving 4¾ cups of sugar in 4 cups water. This amount of syrup will cover approximately 13 pints (6½ quarts) of berries.

—Virginia Department of Agriculture
and Consumer Services

Strawberry Preserves

Yield: 3 half-pint jelly jars

5 cups berries, capped
3 cups sugar

Combine berries and 1 cup sugar in a heavy saucepan. Bring to a boil. Cook 10 minutes, stirring frequently. Stir in remaining sugar and boil an additional 5 minutes, stirring frequently. Pour berry mixture into 13-by-9-by-2-inch pan. Skim off foam. Let stand uncovered in cool place for 12 hours, shaking pan occasionally. *Do not stir.* Pack preserves in hot sterile jars and process in boiling water for 20 minutes. This recipe may be doubled.
—Oliver's Farm Market
Mrs. Gordon Oliver

Russian Strawberry Soup

Yield: 8 servings

2 10-ounce packages frozen strawberries or other berries, or equal amount of fresh
Sugar to taste
1 cup sour cream
½ cup water
1 cup claret or sweet white wine

Defrost berries and blend all ingredients, in several batches, in blender. Heat mixture, slowly, stirring with a wooden spoon. Do not boil. Serve icy cold.
—Michelene Mower

Strawberry Gelatin Salad

Yield: 12 servings

2 large packages
  strawberry-flavored
  gelatin
4 cups boiling water
2 packages unflavored
  gelatin
4 teaspoons cold water
4 10-ounce packages frozen
  or fresh strawberries
2 16-ounce cans crushed
  pineapple, drained
4 large bananas, sliced
1 pint sour cream

Mix strawberry gelatin in boiling water. Soften unflavored gelatin in cold water. Add to strawberry gelatin and mix. Cool slightly. Add strawberries, pineapple, and bananas. When partially jelled, pour about a 1-inch layer of strawberry mixture in a 9-by-13-inch pan, and then a thin layer of sour cream. Repeat layers. Chill in refrigerator until completely jelled before serving.
—Mary Martin
Martin's Strawberry Farm

Strawberry Fruit Salad or Dessert

Yield: 4 servings

1 3-ounce package cream
  cheese, at room
  temperature
½ cup heavy cream
2 tablespoons
  confectioner's sugar
¼ teaspoon vanilla extract
2 pints strawberries, washed
  and hulled
Confectioner's sugar as
  needed

In medium bowl, beat cheese with mixer until fluffy. Add cream, sugar, and vanilla. Beat until mixture holds a shape. Mound in crystal bowl and serve as dressing for strawberries. Sprinkle berries with confectioner's sugar and serve.
—Betty Michelson

Strawberry Forgotten Cake

Yield: 1 9-inch cake

1 quart strawberries
12 egg whites (2 cups, plus 4 tablespoons)
½ teaspoon salt
1 teaspoon cream of tartar
2 cups sugar
1 teaspoon vanilla extract
2 cups heavy cream
2 tablespoons confectioner's sugar
Shaved chocolate as needed

Preheat oven to 450 degrees F. Set aside six whole berries for garnish. Slice remaining berries and sprinkle with sugar. Beat whites well. Add salt, cream of tartar, and sugar slowly. Beat until very stiff. In pie pans or cookie sheets shape out three 9-inch meringues. Place in oven. Turn off oven and leave in overnight or at least 5 hours. *Do not open oven door.* Whip cream, adding sugar, until stiff. Make a layer of meringue. Add a layer of strawberries, a layer of meringue, a layer of strawberries, and a layer of meringue. Ice all three layers with the whipped cream. Garnish with whole strawberries and shaved chocolate. Chill for at least 1 hour.

—Eleanor Dunn

Old-Fashioned Strawberry Shortcake

Eileen Boush Davis, whose descendants go back to the early days of Princess Anne County, remembers the strawberry shortcake she ate as a little girl. Her mother would make a rich baking powder biscuit, using up to six tablespoons of shortening. Contrary to many shortcake recipes, she added absolutely no sugar. She would slice one-half the berries, sugar them, and warm them up. She then split the hot biscuits and buttered them, pouring warm berries on the bottom halves, replacing the biscuit tops, and pouring more warm berries over all. Topped with whipped cream and garnished with whole strawberries, it was a dessert you could only afford to eat once a year, Mrs. Davis says.

—Eileen Boush Davis

Bavarois aux Fraises

(Strawberry Bavarian Cream)

Yield: 8 servings

2 pints fresh strawberries
1 8-ounce package frozen
   raspberries
2 envelopes unflavored
   gelatin
1 cup sugar
¼ cup brandy (cognac)
1 cup heavy cream,
   whipped into soft peaks

Reserve 8 to 10 of the prettiest strawberries to decorate the bavarois. Hull the rest. Strain frozen raspberries. Reserve the juice and sprinkle gelatin on the juice to soften. Combine brandy and raspberries in blender. Purée. Add strawberries to blender and purée with raspberry-cognac mixture. Pour purée into saucepan; add sugar and gelatin; warm, stirring until gelatin is dissolved—just a few minutes. Refrigerate until mixture is of egg-white consistency. Fold in whipped cream until no traces of white remain. Pour into individual parfaits or a mold rinsed first with cold water. Refrigerate at least 4 hours. Garnish with reserved strawberries. Serve with whipped cream if desired.

—Michelene Mower

The Virginia Beach City Seal
is encircled by an inner wreath of strawberry leaves.
Courtesy of the city of Virginia Beach

Strawberry Dumplings

Yield: 4 to 5 servings

⅓ cup sugar
⅔ cup water
½ teaspoon vanilla extract
1 cup flour, sifted
2 tablespoons sugar
1½ teaspoons baking
  powder
½ teaspoon salt
¼ cup (½ stick) butter or
  margarine
½ cup milk
2 cups fresh strawberries,
  hulled
1 tablespoon sugar

Preheat oven to 450 degrees F. In sauce-pan combine ⅓ cup sugar and water; bring mixture to a boil, reduce the heat, and simmer uncovered for 5 minutes; stir in vanilla. Sift together flour, 2 tablespoons sugar, baking powder, and salt; cut in margarine until mixture is crumbly; add milk and stir just until combined. Arrange berries in 1½-quart casserole; pour hot sugar mixture over berries; immediately drop dumpling dough in 8 to 10 spoonfuls over berries; sprinkle dumplings with 1 tablespoon sugar. Bake 25 to 30 minutes or until dumplings are done. Serve warm from casserole.

—Shelby Webster

Godiva-Dipped Strawberries

The Ragged Robin is the oldest gift shop at the beach. It recently has begun to stock an assortment of fine foods, such as Godiva Chocolates. Princess Anne County strawberries and chocolate make a heaven-sent combination.

Yield: 1 quart of chocolate strawberries

8 ounces Godiva
  Sweetened Chocolate for
  the Kitchen
¾ cup heavy cream
1 heaping teaspoon
  vegetable shortening
1 teaspoon instant coffee
2 tablespoons orange
  curacao
Dash ground cinnamon
1 quart strawberries,
  washed and dried

Melt chocolate in double boiler over sim-mering water. Add cream, shortening, coffee, curacao, and cinnamon. Mix well and remove from heat. Dip strawberries in chocolate and eat at once or place on waxed paper and allow to dry.

—The Ragged Robin

Strawberry Glacé Pie

Martin's Strawberry Farm on Princess Anne Road has been in business for twenty-five years. Today it is a favorite pick-your-own location. The Martins also raise pick-your-own peaches and grapes on Knotts Island. This is Mary Martin's favorite strawberry pie recipe. In the winter she substitutes frozen strawberries for fresh and cuts down on the amount of water in the recipe.

Yield: 1 9-inch pie

1½ quarts fresh
   strawberries, hulled,
   washed, and drained
1 cup sugar
3 tablespoons cornstarch
½ cup water
1 tablespoon butter or
   margarine
1 9-inch pie shell, baked
1 cup heavy cream,
   whipped
2 tablespoons sifted
   confectioner's sugar

Crush with potato masher enough of the berries to make 1 cup. Combine sugar and cornstarch in a pan and add crushed berries and water. Cook over medium heat, stirring constantly, until mixture comes to a boil. Continue cooking and stirring over low heat for 3 minutes or until the mixture is thickened and translucent. Remove from heat and stir in butter. Cool. Place the rest of the berries in the pie shell, reserving a few pretty ones for garnishing. Pour cooked berry mixture over berries in the shell and chill 2 hours. Blend whipped cream and sugar. Serve pie topped with whipped cream and garnished with remaining whole berries.

—Mary Martin
Martin's Strawberry Farm

Round Strawberry Shortcake

Bayville Farms is a familiar historic landmark off Shore Drive. The land, part of an original grant to Adam Thoroughgood, and the eighteenth-century manor house at Bayville are protected by the Virginia Outdoors Foundation and the Virginia Historic Landmarks Commission. Dorcas Boudreau and her husband are employees of the farm. Living there, they especially enjoy the fruits of the land.

Yield: 6 servings

3 cups flour
½ cup sugar
Pinch salt
1 egg
½ cup (1 stick) butter, at
    room temperature
½ to ¾ cups milk
1½ teaspoons baking
    powder

Preheat oven to 425 degrees F. Mix all ingredients well and bake in a greased 8- or 9-inch round cake or pie pan for 15 to 20 minutes until done. Brush top with melted butter. Split in half lengthwise. Fill with strawberries and top with strawberries and whipped cream.

—Dorcas Boudreau
Bayville Farms

Watermelon Rind Pickle—
Old Donation Church

This recipe belongs to Old Donation Episcopal Church. It is included in their cookbook, *Bell Ringer Recipes of Old Donation,* and is a big seller at the church's fall bazaar and oyster roast. Old Donation is the only colonial church remaining in Virginia Beach. Prior to the Revolutionary War, a parish was established when the first church, or "mother church," was built. Adam Thoroughgood built Lynnhaven Parish's mother church in 1639 near his home on the western branch of the Lynnhaven River. This church eventually evolved into Old Donation which was built circa 1736. Gutted by fire in the late 1800s, Old Donation was rebuilt in 1916.

OLD DONATION CHURCH
VIRGINIA BEACH, VIRGINIA

Old Donation Church, built around 1736, is the only remaining colonial church in Princess Anne County. Gutted by fire in 1882, it has been restored. Pen and ink by Janice O. Dool

---

Yield: 4 quarts

7 pounds watermelon rind, peeled
1 pound Lily's Lime
5 pounds sugar
1½ sticks cinnamon
1 teaspoon whole allspice
1½ pints vinegar
1½ teaspoons whole cloves
4 small ginger roots

Soak rind with lime overnight in water to cover. Rinse twice in cold water. Boil rind 15 minutes in fresh water. Drain. Make syrup of 2 quarts of water and sugar and spices contained in a cheesecloth bag. Add rind and more water to cover. Simmer rind in syrup for 1 hour. Seal in sterilized jars.

—Old Donation Episcopal Church
Bell Ringer Recipes of Old Donation,
1976

Watermelon Rind Pickles Whitehurst

Yield: about 6 pints

1 medium-sized watermelon
  rind
1 bottle powdered lime
1 quart apple cider vinegar
5 pounds sugar
1 ounce cinnamon sticks
1 ounce whole cloves

Peel outside and remove all red from inside watermelon rind. Cut in small pieces and soak overnight in lime water (one bottle lime to enough water to cover rind). Next morning remove rind; don't wash. Cover in clear water. Cook 2 hours. Remove and drain well. Make syrup of vinegar and sugar; add cinnamon sticks, and cloves tied in cheesecloth. Add syrup to rind and boil 1 hour. Remove cheesecloth with spices. Pack hot in jars.

Note: Lime may be purchased at any drugstore.

—Edith Whitehurst

Watermelon Pickles Murden

Yield: 4 pints

2 pounds watermelon rind
¼ cup salt
1 quart water
2 pounds sugar
1 pint vinegar
1 teaspoon ground
  cinnamon
1 teaspoon allspice
1 lemon, thinly sliced

Soak watermelon rind overnight in salt water. Drain off the brine and cook the watermelon rind in clear water until it is tender. Add the rind to hot pickling ingredients and boil rapidly until it becomes clear.

—Mrs. Lloyd Murden
What's Cooking at Charity
Charity United Methodist Church, 1962

38

Watermelon Pickles Wise

Yield: 6 pints

1 watermelon (5½ pounds
   rind)
4 tablespoons salt
3 tablespoons powdered
   alum
5½ pounds (11 cups) white
   sugar
2 cups white vinegar
1½ tablespoons whole
   cloves
3 sticks cinnamon
6 blades mace

Remove all the green skin from the rind and cut it into 2-inch rectangles or triangles. Leave a tiny edge of pink for color. Weigh out 5½ pounds or 4 quarts of rind.

Place rind in 4 quarts cold water with salt. Set aside overnight. Drain and wash carefully. Add alum and 4 quarts water. Bring to a boil, and then reduce heat and simmer 30 minutes. Drain and rinse. Simmer in 4 more quarts of water for about 45 minutes or until tender.

Add enough water to cover rind if needed. Add sugar and cook quickly until rind becomes transparent (about 45 minutes). Add vinegar and cook another 25 minutes. Put in spices and cook just 5 minutes. Longer cooking makes syrup dark. Put in sterilized jars. Fill with syrup and spices. Seal.

—Helen Wise

Frozen Fruit Dessert
(Excellent for a mechanical refrigerator)

Betty Michelson found this recipe in her family's papers. Evidently it came out about the time refrigerators did.

Yield: 4 servings

½ cup diced pineapple
½ cup diced peaches
½ cup diced pears
⅓ cup sugar
1 tablespoon lemon juice
⅔ cup whipped cream

Mix ingredients and pour into a tray in mechanical refrigerator. In about 4 hours the dessert will be frozen. This dessert can also be frozen by packing tightly in a covered mold and burying 4 hours in five parts chopped ice and one part coarse salt.

—*Betty Michelson*

Mary Nash Herbert Hoggard's Grapefruit Salad Dressing

This recipe is as old as the century and requires a little experimentation. It is excellent on grapefruit and avocado salad.

Yield: about 1½ cups

½ cup sugar, just wet with lemon juice
Pinch salt
Cooking oil

Combine sugar, lemon juice, and salt. Beat in oil until mixture jellies. Let dressing sit and beat again before it is served.
—Alice Walter

View of Lynnhaven Bay. Engraving by S. Hill from painting by J. Shaw, 1820. Courtesy of the Virginia State Library

Vegetables

Dining at the Croatan Club

In a prospectus advertising the Croatan Club, a fancy country club proposed for the Dam Neck area in the 1920s, much was made of the Princess Anne County food. The brochure told of "Lynnhaven oysters still dripping with brine from their nearby beds, salt and fresh water game fish just caught and roasted to a brown deliciousness in the seashore sand, plump quail, diamond back terrapins, Smithfield hams, Princess Ann turkeys...honey sweet cantaloupes, watermelons, 'red to the rind,' green vegetables offered fresh from the three crops that this marvelous truck land grows each year—all prepared by the native cooks who alone know how."

Eating, it appeared, would be a prime recreation of the club. Also advertised were special facilities for barbecues, for clam and oyster roasts, and for cooking wild game on a spit, designed to produce a "feast that Lucullus never knew nor dreamed of...." The Croatan Club was never able to make good on its promises because the Depression got in the way of its development. Now Dam Neck Naval Weapons Station is on the site of the once-proposed Croatan Club.

Artichoke Dip

Yield: appetizer for 12

1 16-ounce can artichoke
  hearts
1 cup mayonnaise
1 cup grated Parmesan
  cheese
1½ cups shredded
  mozzarella cheese
1 teaspoon garlic powder

Preheat oven to 350 degrees F. Mix all ingredients together. Place in a 10-by-10-inch pan. Bake for 30 minutes.

—Norma Dunn

Gusha

Yield: appetizer for 12

1 pound fresh mushrooms,
  cleaned and stemmed
1 4-ounce can artichokes
1 4- or 6-ounce can black
  olives
1 4- or 6-ounce can green
  olives
¼ cup green pepper, cut in
  big chunks ½-inch or
  more square
½ cup celery, also cut in big
  chunks

Marinade
¾ cup white vinegar
¾ cup olive oil
¼ cup finely chopped red
  onion
2½ teaspoons Italian
  seasoning herb
1 teaspoon salt
1 teaspoon onion salt
1 teaspoon sugar
½ teaspoon pepper

Combine vegetables and set aside. In a saucepan, combine marinade ingredients and bring to boil; simmer 3 minutes. Pour over vegetable mixture and refrigerate. Serve with Melba toast or crackers. Keeps for weeks.

—Norma Dunn

Asperges Mimosa

Yield: 8 servings

2½ to 3 pounds asparagus
   (or green beans)
Boiling water as needed
Salt as needed
¾ cup olive oil
¼ cup white wine vinegar
2 teaspoons prepared
   mustard (¼ teaspoon
   dried)
2 tablespoons finely
   chopped fresh parsley
2 tablespoons finely
   chopped scallions or
   shallots
2 tablespoons finely
   chopped chives
½ teaspoon tarragon
Pinch chervil
Salt to taste
Freshly ground pepper
2 finely chopped hard-
   cooked eggs

Place asparagus in boiling salted water. Bring back to a boil and cook 7 to 14 minutes (according to size) or until stalk end of asparagus can be pierced with a fork. Drain and refrigerate.

To make dressing, combine all ingredients and pour over asparagus when ready to serve.

—Michelene Mower

Asparagus Tips in Puff Pastry

Yield: 6 servings

2 pounds fresh, thin asparagus (about 6 stalks per person)
6 frozen patty shells
½ cup fresh lemon juice
¼ teaspoon salt
Dash white pepper
1 cup (2 sticks) unsalted butter, chilled and cut into 16 pieces
4 to 6 tablespoons hot liquid from steamed asparagus

Wash and trim asparagus. Tie into six bundles with white kitchen string. Steam bundles until barely tender, reserving liquid. Cut off tips, reserving stalks for soup or salad. Cook patty shells according to directions. Make lemon butter sauce by boiling lemon juice with salt and pepper until reduced to 2 tablespoons. Remove from heat and beat in 2 tablespoons of butter. Set over low heat and beat in remaining butter a piece at a time to make a thick creamy sauce. Remove from heat. Just before serving, beat in asparagus liquid by driblets to warm sauce and correct seasoning. Arrange asparagus, tips up, in patty shells. Spoon sauce over. Garnish with thin slice of lemon.

—Barbara Lyle

Guacamole Dip

Yield: about 2 cups

2 ripe avocados, peeled and seeded
½ medium onion, finely minced
1 tablespoon vinegar
Salt and pepper to taste
⅛ teaspoon chili powder
1 very ripe tomato, peeled and chopped

Beat in blender the avocados, onion, vinegar, and seasonings. Fold in tomato. Serve with your favorite chips.

—Judy Humphries

Avocado Bisque Glacé

Yield: 2 to 3 servings

1 large ripe avocado or
   2 small ones
1 cup plain lowfat yogurt
1 cup chicken broth
1 to 2 tablespoons lemon
   juice
½ teaspoon curry powder
   (or to taste)
½ teaspoon horseradish (or
   to taste)
1 teaspoon salt
Pinch tarragon
Freshly ground pepper to
   taste
2 teaspoons tarragon
   vinegar (optional)

Blend all ingredients and chill. Soup may be served with a dollop of sour cream and crumbled bacon or simply another spoonful of yogurt.

Note: A little more chicken broth may be added if mixture is too thick.

—Michelene Mower

How to Cook Beans

This recipe will do just as well for blackeyed peas, butterbeans, or snap beans. Cora Basnight is the daughter of Elizabeth Harris who owns the Harris Farm on Indian River Road.

Yield: 2 to 3 servings

1 pint blackeyed peas,
   butterbeans, or snap
   beans, shelled and
   washed
1 ounce salt pork
Salt and pepper to taste
¼ teaspoon sugar, if desired

Place the peas or beans in pot with salt pork and simmer for 20 to 30 minutes or until tender. Season with salt, pepper, and sugar.

—Cora Basnight
Harris Farm

Beer Batter for Vegetables

This is Judy Humphries' favorite batter for deep frying vegetables such as squash.

Yield: approximately 2 cups batter

1 egg, beaten
½ can cold beer
Flour as needed
Salt, pepper, and garlic
  powder to taste

Mix egg and beer. Add flour until batter is a little bit thicker than pancake batter. Cut squash in strips. Dip in batter and deep fry until golden brown.

—Judy Humphries

Easy Pickled Beets

Yield: 3 pints

5 to 6 cups beets, cooked,
  peeled, and sliced
1 cup vinegar
1 cup sugar
½ teaspoon cinnamon
  (freshly ground if
  possible)
Pinch salt

Pack beet slices into hot sterilized jars. Combine vinegar, sugar, cinnamon, and salt. Bring to a boil and pour over beets in jars. Seal at once.

—Betty Michelson

Pickled Blackeyed Peas

Yield: 8 servings

2 1-pound cans dried
  blackeyed peas, drained,
  or equal amount fresh
  cooked peas
1 cup vegetable oil
¼ cup wine vinegar
1 garlic clove, peeled
¼ cup thinly sliced onion
½ teaspoon salt
Freshly ground black
  pepper to taste

Place peas in bowl. Mix rest of ingredients well and pour over peas. Taste and add more salt or pepper if desired. Store mixture in jar in refrigerator. Remove garlic bud after one day. Store at least two more days before serving. Serve cold or at room temperature with drinks or as a salad course.

—Suzanne S. Jacobson

Cold Broccoli Soup

Michelene Mower uses this basic recipe for almost any vegetable leftovers. She suggests seasoning spinach soup with curry; asparagus and squash soup with nutmeg.

Yield: 4 to 6 servings

1 10-ounce package frozen, chopped broccoli (cooked) or 1 cup leftover cooked vegetables
1 cup milk
1 cup chicken stock
1 cup heavy cream
Grated onion, chives, or onion salt to taste
Salt and pepper to taste

Blend the first three ingredients in the blender. Stir in cream and seasonings to taste. Chill.

—Michelene Mower

Copper Pennies (Marinated Carrots)

Reba S. McClanan, a member of Virginia Beach City Council, also is known for her fine cooking. Her husband Glenn is a member of the Virginia House of Delegates. When he runs for office, she successfully combines politics and cooking by preparing sample ballots which include a selection of her recipes on the other side. The following is one of the recipes the voters received from the McClanans on election day!

Yield: 8 servings

2 pounds carrots, sliced
1 onion, sliced thin
1 cup chopped celery
1 can tomato soup
1 teaspoon prepared mustard
1 teaspoon Worcestershire sauce
1 cup sugar
½ cup vegetable oil
¾ cup vinegar
Salt and pepper

Cook carrots until almost done. Drain and cool. Mix in onion and celery. Combine remaining ingredients and pour over carrots. Mix well. Cover and refrigerate overnight. Drain to serve. (Will keep several days in refrigerator.)

—Reba S. McClanan

Crunchy Carrot Sticks

Yield: about 1 quart

2 pounds carrots
1½ cups vinegar
1 cup sugar
1 tablespoon pickling spices
1 tablespoon salt
1 1-inch cinnamon stick

Peel carrots. Quarter them lengthwise and cut into 4-inch lengths. In a large pot combine vinegar, sugar, spices, salt, and cinnamon; boil for 5 minutes. Add carrots and cook 10 minutes. Pack carrots into hot sterilized jar. Pour boiling liquid over carrots; seal. Allow to stand two weeks before serving to allow flavors to blend.

—Estelle Freeman
Cookbook by Parents, Teachers and Students of Creeds School, 1981

Fruits of Perfection

"All vegetables for table use—such as lettuce, kale, spinach, turnips, beets, peas, snaps, onions, cucumbers, cabbage, tomatoes and melons—and the potato, Irish and sweet, grow luxuriantly. Apples, peaches, apricots, figs and pears succeed well; and the smaller fruits—raspberries, currants, strawberries and gooseberries—are grown to perfection, while the blackberry, whortleberry and cranberries grow luxuriantly in the wild state in the fields, woods and swamps."

—*America. Homes for Englishmen in the State of Virginia,*
real estate brochure on Princess Anne County, 1872

Country-Style Collards

Yield: 6 servings

2 pounds collards, picked
  over and washed
4 to 5 slices of jowl or
  3 tablespoons ham grease
1 teaspoon baking soda
2 tablespoons sugar
6 to 8 medium potatoes
Salt to taste

Boil a few slices of jowl 15 minutes. Wash collards thoroughly and cut out large stalks. Add baking soda to boiling pot and then put in collards, sugar, salt to taste, and potatoes. Boil 1 hour. Cornmeal dumplings are a good addition to these:

2 cups self-rising cornmeal
½ cup plain flour
2 tablespoons dried milk

Mix cornmeal, flour, and dried milk in bowl. Pour in enough boiling water and mix together so that you will be able to make out in little patties. After collards are cooked and removed into covered dishes, drop dumplings in the boiling pot. Cook 15 minutes.

—Ollie Land
Table Talk from
Tabernacle United Methodist Church, 1974

Collard Quiche

You have to try this to believe it!

Yield: 1 10-inch pie

2 cups thinly sliced onions
1 tablespoon butter
2 cups collards
6 eggs
½ cup heavy cream
Dash nutmeg
1 cup grated Swiss cheese
  or processed cheese
1 large garlic clove, crushed
1 10-inch pie shell, unbaked
Sliced mushrooms or black
  olives for decoration

Preheat oven to 425 degrees F. Sauté onions in butter until limp and pale brown. Steam collards 6 to 10 minutes; drain and chop. Toss cheese and garlic together. Line 10-inch pie pan with your favorite crust. Layer onion and collards in pan. Pour in eggs, cream, and nutmeg mixture. Sprinkle with cheese mix. Sprinkle with salt and pepper and decorate with mushrooms or olives. Bake for 25 to 30 minutes.

—Page Davis

Corn on the Cob

Williams Farm on Newtown Road has long had a reputation for fine fresh vegetables. John Williams is a second-generation farmer on that same land. His wife Mary says the secret to good corn is its freshness and how long it is cooked. "Purchase fresh corn the same day it is to be served," she says.

Shuck, silk, and wash the ears. If cooking in a pressure cooker, place 1 cup of water in the cooker. Arrange ears on the rack so steam can circulate. Do not pack too tightly. Let the steam gauge reach 15 pounds (or start to rock). Remove pan from heat and allow pressure to return to normal. Serve. If using a steamer, Mrs. Williams says to add water to the bottom of the rack. Place ears on end. Cover tightly and steam 7 to 10 minutes. Serve.

—Mary Williams
Williams Farm

Fried Sweet Corn

Yield: 8 half-cup servings

3 strips bacon
1 quart sweet corn, cut off
   the cob
1 tablespoon sugar
Pinch salt

Fry bacon in skillet. Remove bacon, pour in corn, and add sugar and salt to taste. Cook on medium heat about 5 minutes, stirring frequently to keep from burning. Crumble up bacon and stir in almost "done" corn. Remove from heat before corn browns.

—Lois Waterfield

Cora Bonney's Stewed Corn

Yield: 6 servings

6 tender ears corn
⅓ cup sugar
1 teaspoon salt
3 cups water
¼ cup (½ stick) butter or
   margarine
⅓ cup flour

Cut corn from cob, add sugar, salt, water, and butter, and cook over medium heat for about 10 minutes. Mix flour with enough water for thickening. Beat until smooth, and then pour into corn mixture and cook 1 minute longer.

Table Talk from
Tabernacle United Methodist Church, 1974

Corn Pudding

Tabernacle United Methodist Church on Sandbridge Road has a rich heritage stretching back to 1789 when the congregation met in a little building on the present site of the church today. They built their present structure in 1830 and it has recently been completely restored. The active congregation has members who can trace their family activities in the Sunday School Sabbath books which go back as early as 1858. Tabernacle families also have a rich culinary heritage built upon the bountiful Princess Anne County harvests. The church's annual Lotus Festival Luncheon and Colonial Dinner are popular events for those who like good country cooking. The church's cookbooks, *What's Cooking at Tabernacle* and *Country Roads* include fine examples of traditional Princess Anne County recipes. This recipe is a staple of the Colonial Dinner.

Yield: 6 servings

2 tablespoons cornstarch
2 eggs
¾ cup sugar
1 15-ounce can evaporated
  milk
1½ pints fresh or frozen
  Silver Queen corn
2 tablespoons melted butter

Preheat oven to 325 degrees F. Mix cornstarch, eggs, and sugar thoroughly. Add milk and corn and mix. Pour into 2-inch deep casserole. Pour melted butter on top. Bake for 1 hour or until firm in middle.

—Etta Mae Land

Corn Fritters

City Councilwoman Barbara Henley and her husband are the owners of pick-your-own vegetable and strawberry fields on Charity Neck Road and Lynnhaven Road. She says these corn fritters are especially good buttered.

Yield: 4 servings

1 cup fresh, tender corn
½ cup milk
½ cup flour
1 teaspoon baking powder
1 teaspoon salt
1 teaspoon melted butter
1 egg
Dash pepper

Mix ingredients well. Drop by spoonfuls onto hot, greased griddle and fry until golden. Serve hot.

—Barbara Henley
Henley Farm

55

Corn Relish

Yield: about 8 pints

9 ears corn
1 medium cabbage
2 medium onions, chopped
3 red peppers
2 green peppers
1 quart vinegar
1 cup sugar
1 teaspoon salt
1½ tablespoons dry mustard
1 teaspoon turmeric

Cook corn in boiling water for 2 minutes. Dip in cold water and cut grains from the cob. Chop the cabbage, onion, and peppers into small pieces and add to corn. Mix vinegar, sugar, salt, and spices and heat to boiling. Add the corn and vegetables and boil until tender, 20 to 30 minutes, stirring frequently. Pour into sterile jars and seal.

—Susan Clark
Cookbook by Parents, Teachers, and Students of Creeds School, 1981

Cold Cucumber Soup

Yield: 6 servings

2 cucumbers, peeled and sliced
2 spring onions, chopped
1 bay leaf
2 tablespoons butter or margarine
3 cups chicken stock
1 cucumber, peeled, seeded, and grated
1 cup half-and-half cream
Juice of ½ lemon
1 teaspoon chopped fresh dill

Sauté cucumbers, onion, and bay leaf in butter until tender. Add chicken stock and simmer for 30 minutes. Cool slightly. Remove bay leaf. Blend in electric blender and strain through a sieve. Chill. Add grated cucumber, cream, lemon juice, and dill. Chill again and serve in chilled soup cups.

Note: Double this recipe when cucumbers are in season and freeze one-half of the base (about 1 quart). Add grated cucumber, cream, lemon, and dill when defrosted and ready to use.

—Mary Reid Barrow

Cucumber Aspic

Yield: 8 to 10 servings

2 envelopes unflavored
   gelatin
2½ cups water, divided
4 medium cucumbers,
   peeled, seeded, and
   grated
1 tablespoon sugar
1 medium onion, grated
1 cup vinegar
Salt and pepper to taste

Soften gelatin in ½ cup cold water. Bring 2 cups water to a boil. Add gelatin and dissolve. Cool. Let grated cucumbers stand for a few minutes and drain off excess liquid. Add cucumbers, sugar, onion, and vinegar to gelatin. Pour in mold. Refrigerate.

—Odie Kellam

Fresh Cucumber Salad

Yield: 8 servings

4 medium cucumbers
½ cup sugar
1 tablespoon salt
½ teaspoon white pepper
½ cup white wine vinegar
½ cup snipped fresh dill or
   2 tablespoons dried dill
   weed

Cut cucumbers crosswise into $\frac{1}{16}$-inch slices; place in bowl with tight fitting lid. Mix sugar, salt, and pepper; sprinkle over cucumbers. Pour vinegar over cucumbers; cover. Refrigerate at least 24 hours. Sprinkle with dill and toss before serving.

—Mary Cooper
Country Roads Cookbook
Tabernacle United Methodist Church, 1981

Marinated Cucumbers

Yield: 1 quart

1 onion, sliced
4 to 6 cucumbers
1 cup sugar
1 cup vinegar

Place sliced onions in a quart jar. Score sides of unpeeled cucumbers with fork. Slice thinly; add to jar. (Should fill jar.) Bring sugar and vinegar to a boil and pour over cucumbers and onions. Cool; cover and refrigerate until chilled. Will last several days in refrigerator.

—Madge Taylor
Cookbook by Parents, Teachers, and Students of Creeds School, 1981

Bread and Butter Pickles

Charity Neck Methodist Church had its roots in the late 1700s as "Dawley's Meetinghouse." Located in the Pungo area of the county, the little church had its name, "Charity," and a building of its own by the end of the century. Following the Civil War, there was a great deal of dissension among its members because a brother was selling some of those good Princess Anne County vegetables in Norfolk on the Sabbath! The church has been destroyed by fire twice, and the present structure was built in 1941. Proceeds from their cookbook, *What's Cooking at Charity,* go into the church building fund.

Yield: 8 pints

1 gallon medium
  cucumbers, sliced
8 small white onions, sliced
1 green pepper
1 cup salt
Cracked ice as needed
5 cups sugar
1½ tablespoons turmeric
1½ teaspoons ground
  cloves
2 tablespoons mustard seed
5 cups vinegar
2 tablespoons celery seed

Combine cucumbers and onion. Cut peppers in narrow strips and add to mixture. Add salt; cover with cracked ice. Mix thoroughly. Let stand 3 hours. Drain. Combine remaining ingredients. Pour over cucumber mixture. Bring to a boil. Seal in sterilized jars.

—Mary Ackiss
What's Cooking at Charity, 1962

Freezer No-Cook Pickles

Yield: about 6 pints

7 cups thinly sliced
   cucumbers
3 small onions, sliced
1 green pepper, sliced
2 cups sugar
½ teaspoon celery seed
1 cup vinegar
1 tablespoon canning salt

Mix all ingredients together. Pack in containers and freeze. Allow to thaw before serving.

—Margaret Hood

Sweet Pickles

Yield: about 12 quarts

7 pounds cucumbers (add
   1 cucumber for the ends)
2 cups hydrated lime to
   1 gallon water
5 pounds sugar, divided
2 quarts vinegar
2 tablespoons pickling
   spices
1 tablespoon celery seed
1 teaspoon salt

Wash and slice cucumbers; soak in lime solution for 24 hours. Soak again in clear water about 3 hours. Drain and soak up excess water with a towel. Set aside 1 cup of sugar. Add remaining sugar, vinegar, pickling spices, celery seed, and salt. Let stand for 12 hours and then boil for 45 minutes. Seal in sterilized jars.

—Lillie James
Table Talk from
Tabernacle United Methodist Church, 1974

Dill Crock

Use a gallon-sized stone crock. Peel several garlic cloves and place in the bottom of the crock. Add ⅔ cup of salt, 9 cups of water, ½ cup vinegar, and a bunch of fresh dill. Add fresh vegetables to your liking, such as sliced firm green tomatoes, cauliflower florets, sliced cucumbers, carrots, and onions. Within a few days the vegetables, still crisp, will be spicy with the dill flavor.

—Louisa Venable Kyle

Fried Eggplant with Green Peppers

Yield: 6 servings

1¾ cups olive oil, divided
4 medium tomatoes, peeled,
  seeded, and coarsely
  chopped
2 large garlic cloves, peeled
  and thinly sliced
1 teaspoon plus ¼ cup salt,
  divided
1 medium (1 pound)
  eggplant
1 quart water
2 medium green peppers,
  cut lengthwise in quarters

Heat 2 tablespoons of olive oil. Add tomatoes, garlic, and 1 teaspoon salt. Cook to a thick purée. Peel eggplant; cut lengthwise into ½-inch thick slices. Lay each slice flat and cut lengthwise strips at ½-inch intervals, starting at the wide end and cutting within 2 inches of the narrow end. It should look like a fan. Soak eggplant for 10 minutes in the quart of water and ¼ cup salt.

Heat remaining olive oil and fry three or four slices at a time until golden brown, 5 minutes on each side; drain on paper towels.

Add green pepper, skin side up. Cook on moderate heat for about 10 minutes. Drain and peel off skin with knife. Mound eggplant in the center of serving platter; pour sauce over it and arrange pepper around it. Serve at room temperature.

—Sandy Lapchick

Italian Eggplant Casserole

Yield: 12 servings

1 very large or 2 medium
    eggplants, pared and cut
    in 1-inch cubes
Salted water as needed
1 pound roll sausage
1 large onion, chopped
1 large green pepper,
    chopped
2 8-ounce cans tomato
    sauce
½ teaspoon oregano
1 teaspoon basil
½ teaspoon salt
1 tablespoon sugar
1½ cups buttered
    breadcrumbs
¾ cup grated mozzarella or
    sharp cheese

Preheat oven to 350 degrees F. Parboil eggplant in salted, boiling water until barely tender. Drain well. In a large skillet, crumble sausage and cook until brown. Remove sausage with slotted spoon into buttered 9-by-13-inch casserole. Pour off all but 3 tablespoons of the drippings in the skillet. Sauté onion and pepper until tender. Add tomato sauce and seasonings to the skillet. Mix well. Gently fold in eggplant. Pour mixture into casserole and mix with sausage. Sprinkle with breadcrumbs and cheese. Bake about 30 minutes.

Note: Zucchini squash can be substituted for eggplant. Don't parboil or pare the zucchini.

—Mary Jane Borchers

Stuffed Eggplant

Yield: 4 servings

1 large eggplant
1 pound lean hamburger
1 green pepper, seeded and
    chopped
1 medium onion, chopped
½ teaspoon garlic salt
Pepper as needed
½ teaspoon oregano
½ cup breadcrumbs
1 tablespoon butter

Preheat oven to 350 degrees F. Cut eggplant in half. Scoop out centers, chop, and reserve. Leave about ¼-inch shells. Parboil shells until just tender but still holding their shapes. Fry hamburger until brown. Add onion and pepper and cook until tender. Drain. Mix with eggplant and seasonings. Fill eggplant shells with mixture. Top with breadcrumbs and butter. Bake 25 to 30 minutes.

—Mary Williams
Williams Farm

Eggplant Parmigana

Yield: 4 servings

3 tablespoons melted butter or margarine
½ cup corn flake crumbs
¼ cup grated Parmesan cheese
½ teaspoon salt
Dash pepper
1 small eggplant
1 egg, slightly beaten
1 8-ounce can tomato sauce
½ teaspoon dried oregano
½ teaspoon sugar
Dash onion salt
2 ounces grated mozzarella cheese

Preheat oven to 400 degrees F. Pour melted butter into a 10-by-8-by-2-inch baking dish; set aside. Combine corn flake crumbs, Parmesan cheese, salt, and pepper; stir well and set aside. Peel eggplant and cut into ¾-inch slices. Dip each slice in egg and coat with crumb mixture; arrange in baking dish. Bake for 20 minutes; turn slices and bake an additional 15 minutes.

Combine the tomato sauce, oregano, sugar, and onion salt in a small saucepan; bring to a boil, stirring occasionally. Pour sauce over eggplant and top with mozzarella. Bake an additional 3 minutes or until cheese is slightly melted.

—Judy Humphries

Grace Sherwood was the only person in Virginia to be proven a witch by ducking. Drawing by Charles Sibley. Courtesy of the Virginia Beach Maritime Historical Museum

Tidewater Mushroom Farms

Tidewater Mushroom Farms was established in 1958. Until several years ago, it supplied all of Tidewater with big, beautiful mushrooms grown right on the premises. Today, the farm no longer grows its own mushrooms, but the ones it ships into Tidewater still are of the highest quality. Howard E. Jones, president of the company, likes the large mushrooms stuffed with ground Smithfield ham, crabmeat, or sausage, bound with a white sauce, and baked at 350 degrees F. for 10 minutes. He also chops the stems, sautés them in butter, adds breadcrumbs and Parmesan cheese, and stuffs the mixture into mushroom caps.

Munchrooms

Yield: 24 appetizers

½ pound fresh mushrooms, chopped
2 tablespoons butter
½ medium onion, chopped fine
1 3-ounce package cream cheese, at room temperature
1 egg yolk
4 tablespoons melted butter
Salt and pepper to taste
Cocktail rounds

Sauté mushrooms in 2 tablespoons butter and add onion. Take off stove and add cream cheese, egg yolk, melted butter, salt, and pepper. Mix together. Spread on cocktail rounds and broil until golden brown.

—Beth Murray
VA-42. Oceana Naval Air Station
A Flight Plan Before Dinner, 1982

Mushroom Sauce

Yield: 3 cups

2 cups milk
4 tablespoons (½ stick)
    butter, divided
3 tablespoons flour
½ pound mushrooms
½ teaspoon salt
⅛ teaspoon white pepper

Heat milk almost to boiling. In a 1½- or 2-quart saucepan, melt 2 tablespoons butter over low heat. Add flour, and cream them together with a wire whisk. Cook this butter-flour mixture for 2 minutes. Keep stirring with the whisk so it does not brown. Add hot milk (½ cup first, then the rest slowly), stirring with the whisk all the time to make the sauce smooth. Beat the sauce for about 3 minutes and then let it simmer. Stir with the whisk from time to time. While the sauce is simmering, slice ½ pound mushrooms fine on the large blade of a vegetable grater. In a large skillet (12-inch size is the best) heat 2 tablespoons butter until bubbly. Cook the mushroom slices over moderately high heat for about 3 minutes. Stir them often and be careful not to allow them to lump together. Quite a bit of steam will escape. Add the mushrooms to the simmering sauce. Use a rubber scraper to get all the butter out of the frying pan into the sauce. Stir and simmer for 2 more minutes. Add salt and pepper.

Note: One or more of the following seasonings may be added:
    chopped fresh parsley, chives, or watercress
    chopped and sauteed shallots, garlic, onions, or scallions
    1 teaspoon lemon juice or Worcestershire sauce
    some slivers of cooked ham
    1 tablespoon capers
    ⅛ teaspoon basil, cardamom, chervil, coriander, dill, dry mustard,
        fennel, ginger, mace, marjoram, nutmeg, savory, tarragon,
        or thyme
    1 tablespoon dry white wine, sherry, brandy, or dry vermouth
                                    —Howard E. Jones, President
                                    Tidewater Mushroom Farms Inc.

64

Cream of Mushroom Soup

Yield: 4 to 6 servings

This is a pure mushroom cream soup which glorifies the mushrooms in it.
Add 2 more cups of milk to the basic Mushroom Sauce recipe. Spoon a teaspoon of butter into each bowl before serving. For a richer soup, replace some of the milk with cream.

—Howard E. Jones, President
Tidewater Mushroom Farms, Inc.

Mushroom Sauté

This is one of Howard Jones' favorite mushroom recipes. He is president of the Tidewater Mushroom Farms.

Yield: 4 servings

1 stick (½ cup) butter
1 pound mushrooms, sliced
Salt, pepper, paprika, garlic
    powder, chives, and
    parsley to taste

Melt butter. Sauté mushrooms with seasonings for about 10 minutes. Serve with steak or other meat dish.

—Howard E. Jones, President
Tidewater Mushroom Farms

Shamrock Marathon

Over the years the Shamrock Marathon in Virginia Beach has become one of the better known races in the United States. The scenic route through Seashore State Park and down the boardwalk and the superb organization by the Tidewater Striders have both contributed to making the race so popular. Dr. Melvin Williams, director of the Human Performance Laboratory at Old Dominion University, is the local advisor to marathon runners. He recommends a high carbohydrate meal, either pasta or pancakes, the night before a marathon. He says vegetables, salad, and a good dessert are appropriate accompaniments, but meats and other foods that digest slowly should be avoided. The following Princess Anne County pasta would make a good marathon eve dinner. In any case, Dr. Williams says runners should experiment to find out what foods suit them best.

Princess Anne County-Style
Pasta Sauce

Yield: 2 servings

1 onion, sliced
1 garlic clove, minced
2 tablespoons butter
½ green pepper, diced
2 carrots, sliced
1 stalk celery, sliced
1 yellow squash, sliced thin
2 tomatoes, peeled and cut
　　in chunks
1 tablespoon fresh oregano
1 teaspoon fresh thyme
Freshly ground pepper
　　to taste

Sauté onion and garlic in butter. Add pepper, carrots, and celery. Cook for 5 minutes. Add squash, tomatoes, herbs, and pepper. Cook another 5 minutes or until vegetables are of desired tenderness. Toss with fresh pasta and a combination of freshly grated Parmesan and Assiago cheeses.

　　　　　　　　　　　　—Mary Reid Barrow

May Pea Hints

Cook small peas for 6 to 8 minutes in a little water. Season with salt, pepper, butter, and a little half-and-half cream.

—Dorcas Boudreau
Bayville Farm

Season the cooking water with a few leaves of mint.

—Kate Chapman

Cream of Fresh Pea Soup

Gordon Oliver is a second-generation Princess Anne County farmer and his grandfather was a farmer in old Norfolk County. For more than twenty years, Oliver's Farm Market has been a landmark on Haygood Road. This pea soup is one of Mrs. Oliver's favorite recipes.

Yield: 8 servings

1 quart chicken stock
3 pounds fresh peas, shelled
   (about 3 cups)
5 tablespoons unsalted
   butter
¼ cup flour
4 cups hot milk
1 teaspoon salt
¼ teaspoon freshly ground
   white pepper, divided
Sugar to taste (optional)

Freeze peas until hard, about 1 hour. Place peas in blender and purée with on-and-off motion until they look like cornmeal. Heat 3 tablespoons butter. Stir in flour until mixture is smooth. Cook 3 minutes, stirring constantly. Gradually add hot milk, stirring constantly. Lower heat to simmer. Add salt and ⅛ teaspoon pepper. Simmer 10 minutes, stirring occasionally. Meanwhile, heat stock to boiling. Stir in pea purée, reduce heat, and simmer stock about 4 minutes or until peas are soft. Whisk pea mixture into sauce and simmer 10 minutes, stirring occasionally. Taste and adjust seasonings with sugar. Strain soup into serving tureen, swirl in remaining butter, and dust with remaining pepper.

—Oliver's Farm Marker
Mrs. Gordon Oliver

New Potatoes

3 to 4 little new potatoes per
  serving
Fresh chopped chives to
  taste
Butter as needed
Lemon juice to taste
Freshly ground pepper to
  taste

Boil potatoes until tender, 10 to
15 minutes depending on size. Pierce with
ice pick (rather than fork) to test for
doneness. Season with chives, butter,
lemon juice, and pepper.

—Mary Reid Barrow

Irish Potato Biscuits

This is an old family recipe. Elizabeth Cason says the biscuits are special
because they stay soft even when cold.

Yield: about 12 biscuits

1 medium white potato,
  peeled
4 tablespoons vegetable
  shortening
1 cup milk, approximately
2 cups flour, divided
4 teaspoons baking powder
1 teaspoon salt

Boil potato and mash while still hot,
adding shortening and about ½ cup of the
flour. Beat until fluffy. Sift together flour,
baking powder, and salt; add to potato
mixture gradually, adding milk as necessary. Preheat oven to 450 degrees F.
Knead mixture thoroughly until it is
smooth and elastic. Shape into biscuits by
hand and place on greased cookie sheet.
Bake 12 to 15 minutes or until brown.

—Elizabeth Cason

Mrs. McNeil's Pumpkin Pie

Yield: 1 9-inch pie

1 whole pumpkin, seeded
  and pulped
2 eggs, beaten
1 tablespoon flour
1 cup sugar
¼ teaspoon salt
¾ cup milk
2 teaspoons cinnamon
2 teaspoons cloves
2 teaspoons nutmeg
1 9-inch pie shell, unbaked

Cut pumpkin in long slices. Peel the
slices and cut into ¾-inch pieces. Place in
pan and cover three-fourths with water.
Cook until soft. Preheat oven to 350
degrees F. Mash pumpkin with fork until
smooth. Using 1½ cups of the mashed
pumpkin, add eggs, flour, sugar, salt, milk,
and spices. Mix well. Pour into pie shell and
bake about 45 minutes or until set.

—Willa Engel

Farmer's Market

The Farmer's Market on Landstown Road in Virginia Beach is a colorful, old-fashioned outdoor market. Vendors' wares range from fresh fruits and vegetables to seafood, baked goods, honey, candies, flowers, bedding plants, and crafts. Judy Humphries and her husband had a stall where they sold primarily fresh produce they raised themselves, beginning with May peas and continuing with other vegetables such as tomatoes, sweet corn, potatoes, peppers, and a variety of squashes throughout the summer. She shared recipes with her customers, and several of them for zucchini, pumpkin, and butternut squash are included in this book.

Pumpkin Seed Butter

Yield: about 2 cups

½ cup pumpkin seed
½ cup honey
½ cup peanuts
½ cup sesame seeds
2 tablespoons vegetable oil
Salt to taste

Place all ingredients in a blender and mix until desired texture is reached.

Note: This recipe works best with the Lady Godiva variety of pumpkin, as its seeds are "naked," or have no hard outer shell.

—Judy Humphries
*Pumpkin Recipe Ideas from
the Farmer's Market*

Toasted Pumpkin Seeds

Preheat oven to 250 degrees F. Separate seeds from fiber. Cover seeds with salted boiling water. Reduce the heat and simmer gently for 1½ to 2 hours. Spread seeds on cookie sheet and coat with peanut oil, using a pastry brush. Salt to taste and bake until slightly brown.

—Judy Humphries
Pumpkin Recipe Ideas from the Farmer's Market

Curried Rice Salad

Yield: 8 servings

2 cups rice
6 cups chicken stock
1 inch fresh gingerroot
½ teaspoon turmeric
1 teaspoon curry powder
Salt and pepper to taste
½ cup olive oil
Juice of 2 lemons
½ cup white raisins
½ cup currants
1 cup chopped green
   peppers
½ cup mayonnaise
½ cup sour cream
Toasted almonds to taste
Chopped parsley to taste

Cook rice in chicken stock with ginger-root, turmeric, curry, salt, and pepper according to package directions. Toss with olive oil and lemon juice and refrigerate overnight. The day of serving, add raisins, currants, green peppers, mayonnaise, and sour cream. Just before serving, garnish with almonds and parsley.

—Shelby Balderson

Stuffed Acorn Squash

Yield: 4 servings

2 acorn squash
½ cup celery, diced
½ cup carrot, diced
2 tablespoons diced onion
1 tablespoon butter
1 cup cooked ham, diced, *or*
   4 to 5 strips cooked bacon
Salt to taste
Broth or milk as needed

Preheat oven to 350 degrees F. Cut squash in half lengthwise. Bake until tender. Sauté vegetables in butter until soft and add meat. Remove seeds from squash and scoop out pulp. Mash pulp with salt and add broth or milk until a fluffy texture is reached. Combine with vegetables; pack into squash shells or dishes and bake another 15 minutes.

—Judy Humphries
Acorn Squash Ideas from
the Farmer's Market

Baked Acorn Squash

Yield: 2 servings

1 medium acorn squash, cut
   in half lengthwise
1 tablespoon melted butter
¼ cup milk
½ cup maple syrup

Preheat oven to 350 degrees F. Remove seeds and stringy portion of squash. On cookie sheet, place cut-side down and bake for 45 minutes. Turn squash over and fill with remaining ingredients. Bake another 15 minutes.

Note: Brown sugar, crushed pineapple, or applesauce may be used for a sweetener. Do not use milk with these sweeteners.

—Judy Humphries
*Acorn Squash Ideas from
the Farmer's Market*

Deep-Fried Acorn Squash Strips

Yield: 2 servings

1 medium acorn squash
Brown sugar to taste
Allspice to taste

Cut squash into ½-inch thick semi-circles, pared. Fry in deep fat at 360 degrees F. until lightly browned and tender. Drain on paper towel and sprinkle or roll in seasonings.

—Judy Humphries
*Acorn Squash Ideas from
the Farmer's Market*

Baked Cymlings

This was Betty Michelson's grandmother's recipe. Cymlings are the little round white squash with the scalloped edges.

Yield: 4 servings

6 cymlings, stems removed
  and diced
2 onions, peeled and diced
4 tablespoons butter
Salt and pepper to taste

Boil squash and onions until tender. Drain. Preheat oven to 350 degrees F. Layer squash mixture in casserole with butter and seasonings ending with butter on top. Bake 20 minutes or until bubbly.

—Betty Michelson

Baked Squash

Yield: 6 servings

3 pounds yellow crookneck
  squash
½ cup chopped onions
2 eggs
½ cup (1 stick) butter,
  divided
1 tablespoon sugar
1 teaspoon salt
½ teaspoon black pepper
½ cup cracker crumbs

Preheat oven to 375 degrees F. Wash and cut up squash. Boil until tender. Drain thoroughly. Mash. Add onions, eggs, half the butter, sugar, salt, and pepper. Place mixture in baking dish. Melt remaining butter and pour over mixture. Crush crackers and sprinkle over top of mixture. Bake for about 1 hour or until brown on top.

—George M. Ohlinger

Summer Squash Casserole

The Virginia Truck and Ornamentals Research Station in Virginia Beach has been experimenting with yellow squash for years, and the wife of the director has been cooking it in various ways for years, also!

Yield: 6 servings

1 large onion, sliced
½ cup green and/or red
   pepper
2 tablespoons bacon
   drippings, oil, *or* butter
4 medium yellow squash
1 teaspoon salt
1 egg, beaten
½ cup milk
½ cup grated cheese
   (mozzarella, Cheddar, or
   Parmesan)
1 cup coarse buttered
   breadcrumbs

Preheat oven to 350 degrees F. Sauté onion and pepper in drippings in large skillet. Add squash and a small amount of water to prevent sticking. Cover and cook until squash is barely tender. Pour off any excess water. Mash squash with potato masher. Add salt, egg, milk, and half the cheese. Pour mixture into greased 9-inch square pan. Sprinkle with remaining cheese and breadcrumbs. Bake about 30 minutes.

—Mary Jane Borchers

Stir-Fried Young Squash

Pick zucchini and yellow squash while still tiny and tender. Slice in thirds or fourths. Quickly stir-fry in olive oil with garlic and onion. Season with pepper and serve.

Spaghetti Squash

To bake a spaghetti squash, cut it in half and place cut-side down in a baking dish with a small amount of water. Preheat oven to 350 degrees F. and bake until fork tender, about 30 minutes. Scoop out the inside of the squash which will resemble spaghetti. Serve with butter, grated cheese, and/or spaghetti sauce.

—Mary Williams
Williams Farm

Sautéed Squash Blossoms

When the zucchini (or yellow squash) is at its height, pick it when it's very young, barely two inches long, with the blossom still attached, and try this recipe. This is a delicious alternative to all the overgrown zucchini you end up with at the end of the season which is good only for zucchini bread.

Yield: 4 servings

1 dozen 2-inch zucchini
  with blossoms still
  attached
3 tablespoons olive oil
2 garlic cloves, finely
  chopped
Pepper to taste
Lemon juice to taste

Wash squash gently. The blossoms will wilt, but don't worry. Add olive oil to large skillet. Sauté garlic about two minutes. Add whole squash with blossom. Coat with oil and cover pan for 3 minutes or so. Sprinkle with pepper and lemon juice and serve. (If there is disparity in the size of the squash, cut the larger ones in half lengthwise before cooking.)

—Eleanor Dunn

Crisp Squash Pickles

Yield: 4 pints

8 cups thinly sliced yellow
  squash
2 cups chopped (or thinly
  sliced) onions
2 large green peppers,
  chopped
2 tablespoons salt
2 cups vinegar
3 cups sugar
2 tablespoons mustard seed
2 teaspoons celery seed

In a large container, place squash, onions, peppers, and salt. Cover with ice water and set aside 1 hour; drain well. In saucepan combine vinegar, sugar, mustard, and celery seed; bring to a full boil, stirring often to dissolve sugar. Add vegetables and return liquid to full boil. Pack in hot sterilized jars and seal at once.

—Estelle Freeman
*Cookbook by Parents, Teachers,
and Students of Creeds School, 1981*

Zucchini Cora

Yield: 10 servings

3 cups grated zucchini
1 cup biscuit mix
½ cup finely chopped onion
½ cup Parmesan cheese
2 tablespoons chopped
    parsley
½ teaspoon salt
½ teaspoon seasoned salt
½ teaspoon oregano
¼ teaspoon marjoram
1 garlic clove, minced
Dash pepper
½ cup vegetable oil
4 eggs, slightly beaten

Preheat oven to 350 degrees F. Mix first eleven ingredients in a bowl. Mix oil with beaten eggs and stir into zucchini mixture. Pour into greased 13-by-9-by-2-inch pan and bake for 25 to 30 minutes. Serve in squares.

—Willa Engel

Harvest Zucchini

Yield: 4 servings

¼ cup butter
1¼ pounds zucchini, sliced
⅓ cup finely chopped
    onions
½ cup sour cream
2 tablespoons milk
1 teaspoon salt
2 teaspoons paprika
2 teaspoons poppy seed

Melt butter in large skillet. Add zucchini and onion. Stir and cover. Cook, stirring occasionally, until zucchini is tender. Mix remaining ingredients; stir gently into zucchini and heat through.

—Willa Engel

Zucchini Bread

Judy Humphries and her husband had a stall at the Farmer's Market. She suggests peeling, boiling, and mashing butternut squash and substituting it for zucchini in this recipe.

Yield: 2 loaves

2 cups sugar
1 cup vegetable oil
3 eggs
1 teaspoon vanilla extract
2 cups shredded raw
   zucchini (skin and all)
3 cups flour
¼ teaspoon baking powder
1 teaspoon salt
1 teaspoon *each* cinnamon,
   ginger, and ground cloves
1 cup chopped walnuts
1 teaspoon baking soda

Preheat oven to 325 degrees F. Grease and lightly flour two 9-by-5-inch loaf pans. In large mixing bowl combine sugar, oil, eggs, vanilla, and shredded zucchini. Mix well until blended. Sift together flour, baking powder, baking soda, salt, and spices. Add to zucchini and mix until well blended. Stir in chopped nuts and pour into prepared loaf pans. Bake for about 1 hour or until done. Cool in pan about 20 minutes. Remove from pans. Slice when completely cooled. This freezes well.

—Judy Humphries

Sweet Potatoes

In his book, *I Wouldn't Take Nothing for My Journey, Two Centuries of an Afro-American Minister's Family,* Dr. Leonidas H. Berry recalled his stay in Princess Anne County in 1912 to 1914. "The unique and very special Princess Anne cuisine will never be forgotten," he wrote. He particularly remembered the Nancy Hall sweet potatoes, "roasted to a soft consistency and served with natural syrup seeping through the hulls," or "fried or baked into pies or biscuits and other delicious dishes."

Sweet Potato Biscuits

Yield: about 12 biscuits

½ cup sugar
1 teaspoon salt
2 cups self-rising flour
½ cup vegetable shortening
4 medium sweet potatoes,
  baked until soft and
  scooped from shells

Preheat oven to 400 degrees F. Mix sugar and salt with flour. Work shortening into mixture with pastry blender. Work sweet potatoes into flour with blender, adding more flour if necessary to form a light dough. Knead. Roll out on floured board. Cut into biscuits. Bake until tops are brown, about 10 to 12 minutes.

—Lois Waterfield

Sweet Potato Soup

The Virginia Beach Campus of Tidewater Community College is the only state college in Virginia to offer a Culinary Arts Program. This Sweet Potato Soup created especially for a "Made in Virginia" luncheon at the college is an example of the kind of cooking the students learn.

Yield: 6 to 8 servings

2 tablespoons butter
1 medium onion, finely
  chopped
2 tablespoons flour
1 to 3 tablespoons curry
  powder
3 cups chicken broth
1 23-ounce can sweet
  potatoes, or equal
  amount fresh sweet
  potatoes, cooked, peeled
  and mashed
1 cup light cream or 1 cup
  plain yogurt

In hot butter, sauté onion until golden and soft; blend in flour to form a thin paste; stir in curry powder. Add chicken broth and stir until smooth; remove pan from heat. Purée sweet potatoes in small batches in food processor or blender (add some of the chicken broth mixture when using blender) until completely smooth. Stir purée into soup; refrigerate until well chilled. Just before serving add cream and stir well. (If you use yogurt, the flavor will be different.)

—From "Made in Virginia" luncheon
by Culinary Arts students at the
Virginia Beach Campus of
Tidewater Community College

Sweet Potato Casserole

Yield: 6 to 8 servings

3 cups mashed cooked and
   peeled sweet potatoes
1 cup sugar
½ teaspoon salt
2 eggs
4 tablespoons melted butter
   or margarine
½ cup milk
½ teaspoon vanilla extract

Combine all ingredients and mix. Place in a 8- or 9-inch baking dish.

Topping
½ cup brown sugar
¼ cup flour
½ cup chopped nuts of your
   choice
2 tablespoons melted butter
   or margarine

Preheat oven to 350 degrees F. Combine all ingredients and sprinkle over sweet potato mixture. Bake 40 to 45 minutes.
—Judy Humphries

French Fried Sweet Potatoes

Sweet potatoes as desired
1 tablespoon sugar
¼ teaspoon cinnamon
¼ teaspoon salt

Boil sweet potatoes for 10 minutes. Peel and cut into french fries. Fry in deep fat at 375 degrees F. for 3 minutes or until fork tender and golden brown. Drain on paper toweling. Sprinkle with a mixture of sugar, cinnamon, and salt. Serve immediately.
—Virginia Department of Agriculture
and Consumer Services

Glazed Sweet Potatoes

Yield: 6 servings

5 medium sweet potatoes,
    cooked, peeled, and
    sliced lengthwise
Cinnamon to taste
Nutmeg to taste
Grated peel of 1 orange
½ cup dark corn syrup
½ cup orange juice
2 tablespoons butter

Preheat oven to 350 degrees F. Arrange potatoes in greased, shallow casserole dish. Sprinkle with cinnamon, nutmeg, and orange peel. Mix corn syrup and orange juice and pour over potatoes. Dot with butter. Bake for 30 minutes.

—Mary Jane Borchers

Old Virginia Sweet Potato Pie

Yield: 1 9-inch pie

2 eggs
¾ cup sugar
2½ cups milk
½ teaspoon nutmeg
½ teaspoon cinnamon
2 cups mashed cooked
    and peeled sweet
    potatoes
2 tablespoons melted butter
Grated peel of 1 lemon
1 9-inch pie shell, unbaked

Preheat oven to 425 degrees F. Beat the eggs, adding sugar, milk, and spices. Mix mashed potatoes with butter while potatoes are still hot. Add remaining ingredients to sweet potatoes. Pour the mixture into the pie shell and bake for 10 minutes. Reduce heat to 350 degrees F. and bake 30 minutes. While pie is warm, sprinkle surface with granulated sugar, which melts to form a glaze.

—*Country Treasures from Virginia
Farm Bureau Kitchens,* 1982

Grated Sweet Potato Pudding

Yield: 8 servings

4 cups powdered milk
4 sweet potatoes, peeled
   and grated
½ cup light brown sugar
½ cup (1 stick) butter
3 eggs
1¼ cup sugar
Pinch salt
Nutmeg to taste
1 teaspoon lemon or other
   flavoring

Preheat oven to 350 degrees F. Mix powdered milk and scald 2 cups of it. Pour over grated sweet potatoes. Add brown sugar and butter to hot potatoes; beat eggs and add white sugar to eggs. Add this to the potato mixture with the salt and remaining cold milk. Mix well. Add flavoring. Pour into greased baking dish and bake about 1 hour or until set and brown.

—Eva Land
Table Talk from
Tabernacle United Methodist Church, 1974

Sweet Potato Rolls

Yield: 4 dozen rolls

3 cups mashed cooked
   and peeled sweet
   potatoes
1 cup sugar
½ cup warm water
2 packages dry yeast
4 cups plain flour
½ cup vegetable shortening

Mash warm sweet potatoes, adding sugar while warm. Blend the warm water and yeast and pour into sweet potato mixture, mixing well. Then mix flour and shortening together by cutting shortening into flour. After flour and shortening have been mixed well, add to sweet potato mixture and knead. Mixture may need more flour in order to be handled. Let rise until double in size. Then make rolls and let rise about 2 hours or until they have risen as you like them. Preheat oven to 450 degrees F. Bake about 20 minutes or until well browned.

—Elizabeth Eaton

Cold Fresh Tomato Soup

Yield: 4 servings

6 ripe tomatoes, skinned,
    cut in half, squeezed to
    remove seeds, and
    chopped coarsely
1 small onion, finely
    chopped
1 shallot, finely chopped
Few small, fresh basil
    leaves, finely chopped, *or*
    ¼ teaspoon dried basil
Salt and freshly ground
    pepper to taste
1 teaspoon sugar
½ cup dry vermouth, *or*
    dry white wine (optional)
Thin slices unpeeled
    cucumbers for garnish
Sour cream as needed
Fresh chives or dill,
    chopped

Place tomatoes in top of double boiler. Add onion, shallot, basil, salt, pepper, and sugar. Cover and steam over gently simmering water for 15 minutes. Pour mixture into a blender and purée. Add vermouth. Chill several hours. Add thinly sliced cucumbers and 1 tablespoon sour cream sprinkled with dill or chives to each cup when serving.

—Anne Gilliam

Tomato and Zucchini Soup

Yield: 6 servings

1 medium onion, chopped
2 tablespoons vegetable oil
2 small zucchini, finely
    diced
4 cups tomato juice
2 cups chicken broth
3 tablespoons lemon juice
2 teaspoons Worcestershire
    sauce
1 teaspoon salt
⅛ to ¼ teaspoon Tabasco
    sauce
2 tablespoons chopped
    parsley

Sauté onion in oil in large saucepan until soft, about 5 minutes. Stir in zucchini; sauté 2 to 3 minutes. Add remaining ingredients. Heat to boiling, lower heat, and cover. Simmer 5 minutes. Serve hot in mugs.

—Madge Taylor
Cookbook by Parents, Teachers, and Students of Creeds School, 1981

Gazpacho

Yield: 6 servings

1 cup finely chopped peeled
  tomato
½ cup *each* finely chopped
  green pepper, celery, and
  cucumber
¼ cup finely chopped onion
2 teaspoons parsley
1 teaspoon chives
1 small garlic clove, minced
2 to 3 tablespoons tarragon
  wine vinegar
2 tablespoons olive oil
1 teaspoon salt
¼ teaspoon pepper
½ teaspoon Worcestershire
  sauce
2 cups tomato juice

Combine ingredients in stainless steel or glass bowl. Cover and chill at least 4 hours. Serve in chilled cups with croutons.

—Nancy Lowe

Basil Tomato Salad

Yield: 6 servings

½ cup red wine vinegar
⅓ cup olive oil
3 tablespoons fresh basil
1 tablespoon fresh tarragon
1 teaspoon fresh oregano
4 teaspoons sugar
Freshly ground pepper to
  taste
6 beefsteak tomatoes, sliced
2 red onions, thinly sliced

Combine vinegar, oil, basil, tarragon, oregano, sugar, and pepper in bowl and blend well. Layer tomatoes and onions in serving bowl and cover with dressing. Chill until ready to serve.

—Mary Reid Barrow

Marinated Tomatoes

Betty Michelson says this is not really a recipe but was popular, so she's been told, with her great-grandmother's family at "Woodland" because all the ingredients were grown on the farm.

Marinate sliced fresh tomatoes in vinegar diluted with a little water and flavored with a little sugar. Marinate sliced fresh cucumbers and chopped spring onions in the same way but in another bowl. Cook small tender string beans with a little salt pork. Drain and cool and combine all ingredients for a tasty vegetable combination.

—Betty Michelson

Green Tomato Pickle

Yield: about 4 quarts

1 gallon green tomatoes
6 large onions
½ cup salt
½ lemon
3 pods red pepper
2 tablespoons whole cloves
1 tablespoon allspice
1 tablespoon crushed celery
　seed
1 tablespoon mustard seed
1 tablespoon whole black
　peppercorns
3 cups brown sugar
3 cups vinegar

Slice the tomatoes and onions thin. Sprinkle with salt and let stand overnight in a crock or enameled vessel. Slice the lemon and two pepper pods very fine. Tie the cloves, allspice, celery seed, mustard seed, and black pepper in a cheesecloth bag. Drain the tomatoes and onions well. Add seasonings and sugar to vinegar along with tomato and onion mixture. Cook for ½ hour stirring gently at intervals. Remove spice bag. Pack in clean jars and garnish with slender strips of red pepper placed vertically on opposite sides of jars. Process for 15 minutes.

—Betty Michelson

Fried Green Tomatoes

Mrs. Oliver uses this same recipe with 2 pounds of okra, cut into rings.

Yield: 4 servings

4 large, firm green
 tomatoes, sliced in ¼-inch
 slices
½ cup flour and cornmeal
 combined
1 teaspoon salt
Bacon drippings or
 vegetable oil as needed

Dredge tomato slices in cornmeal and seasonings. Sauté in oil until tomatoes are brown, turning once. Drain on paper towels.

-Oliver's Farm Market
Mrs. Gordon Oliver

Sallie's Green Tomato Pie

Yield: 1 8-inch pie

3 or 4 green tomatoes,
 peeled and chopped
2 tablespons vinegar
2 tablespoons water
1 cup sugar
Pinch salt
2 tablespoons flour
1 teaspoon cinnamon
¼ teaspoon allspice
½ teaspoon ground cloves
1 8-inch pie shell, unbaked

Preheat oven to 400 degrees F. Squeeze liquid from tomatoes. Discard juice. Add vinegar and water to tomatoes. Sift sugar with salt, flour, and spices. Mix with tomatoes. Pour into pie shell. Dot with butter. Bake for 15 minutes at 400 degrees F. Reduce heat to 350 degrees F. and bake for 30 minutes more.

—Ruth Barrow

Galilee Bazaar Salad

This salad is a favorite at Galilee Episcopal Church bazaar luncheons. Galilee had its origins in the Bishop Beverly D. Tucker's beach cottage where he conducted services for early oceanfront residents until an inter-denominational chapel was built in 1891. Four years later the chapel became a mission of Eastern Shore Chapel Episcopal Church and was named Galilee Chapel by the Sea. Today, the church is at Forty-ninth Street and Pacific Avenue.

Yield: 12 servings

2 3-ounce packages lime-flavored gelatin
3 cups water
Juice of 1 lemon
1 cup cottage cheese
1 cup mayonnaise, divided
2 tablespoons grated cucumber
1 cup ground cucumber
1 tablespoon grated onion
Pinch pepper and salt

Dissolve one package gelatin in 1½ cups hot water. When cool and slightly congealed, add cottage cheese, ½ cup mayonnaise, grated cucumber, and lemon juice. Pour into an 8-by-8-inch pan and let sit. Dissolve second package of gelatin in 1½ cups hot water. When cool and slightly congealed, add ground cucumber, remaining mayonnaise, onion, salt, and pepper. Pour over cheese mixture and refrigerate until completely set.

—*Loaves and Fishes, II*
Galilee Episcopal Church

Galilee Vegetable Salad Sandwich Spread

This is another Galilee Church luncheon favorite.

Yield: 4 cups

1 envelope unflavored gelatin
¼ cup water
1 cup finely diced celery
1 onion, diced fine
2 small carrots, diced fine
½ green pepper, diced fine
1 teaspoon salt
2 cups mayonnaise

Soak gelatin in water in a small cup until softened. Melt by putting cup in pan of hot water. Mix all other ingredients. Add melted gelatin. Refrigerate until congealed. Use as a sandwich spread.

Loaves and Fishes, II
Galilee Episcopal Church

Vegetable Salad

Mary Jane Borchers, wife of the director of the Virginia Truck and Ornamentals Research Station in Virginia Beach, experiments with many different combinations of fresh, crisp vegetables in this salad.

Yield: 12 servings

1 6-ounce package lime-flavored gelatin
Juice and grated peel of 1 fresh lime
1½ cups thinly shredded cabbage
3 large carrots, coarsely grated
1 small onion, chopped
2 ribs celery, thinly sliced
1 green pepper, seeded, quartered, and sliced
¼ cup snipped parsley

Dissolve gelatin in 2 cups boiling water. Add 2 cups cold water plus juice and peel of lime. Mix vegetables and sprinkle with a little salt. Add to gelatin. Pour into a 9-by-13-inch dish. Refrigerate until firm.

Note: Other vegetables may include pimiento, green olives, cucumber, squash, broccoli, and cauliflower.

—Mary Jane Borchers

Garlic Herb Dressing

Yield: ⅓ cup

1 garlic clove, peeled and crushed
¼ cup olive oil
2 tablespoons red wine vinegar
½ teaspoon tarragon
½ teaspoon marjoram
½ teaspoon dry mustard
¼ teaspoon salt
⅛ teaspoon pepper

In small jar combine all ingredients; tighten lid and shake well. Let stand at room temperature at least 1 hour. Shake again and pour over tossed salad ingredients.

—From "Made in Virginia" luncheon by Culinary Arts students at the Virginia Beach Campus of Tidewater Community College

Mixed Green Vegetables

Fort Story, established in 1914, was known as the "American Gibraltar" during World War I. Today, the Army's amphibious branch uses the fort's natural terrain for training. The Cape Henry Memorial Cross and both of the Cape Henry lighthouses are on Fort Story property. Post Commander Colonel James C. Blewster and his wife live in the Cape Henry House, built on the base in 1918. This is their favorite vegetable recipe.

Yield: 8 servings

1 10-ounce package frozen green peas, or equal amount fresh
1 10-ounce package frozen baby limas, or equal amount fresh
1 10-ounce package frozen cut green beans, or equal amount fresh

Cook and season according to package directions.

Sauce
1 cup mayonnaise
1 teaspoon mustard
3 hard-cooked eggs, grated
2 dashes hot sauce
1 medium grated onion
1 teaspoon Worcestershire sauce
2 tablespoons vegetable oil

Mix all ingredients together and store in refrigerator. Drain hot vegetables and pour sauce over just before serving. Mix gently. This is delicious served with all meat dishes.

—Mrs. James C. Blewster
Fort Story

Poppy Seed Dressing

Yield: about 2 cups

¾ cup sugar
1 teaspoon salt
1 teaspoon dry mustard
⅓ cup vinegar
1 cup vegetable oil
2 teaspoons onion juice
1 tablespoon poppy seed

Mix sugar, salt, and mustard. Add vinegar, oil, onion juice, and poppy seed. Blend well.

—Ruth Barrow

Seafood

Cape Henry Lighthouse
Virginia Beach, Virginia

© Janice O. Dool, 1972

The Cape Henry Lighthouse, built in 1789, is owned by the Virginia
Association for the Preservation of Virginia Antiquities. Located at Fort Story,
it is open to the public. Pen and ink by Janice O. Dool

Dining at the Virginia Beach Hotel

The Virginia Beach Hotel, predecessor to the elegant Princess Anne Hotel, reached a peak of elegance all its own in 1885 when it served a banquet in honor of the United States Minister to Brazil, Thomas J. Jarvis and 100 other dignitaries, including the governors of Virginia and North Carolina.

The head table, gaily decorated with flowers, ran the entire length of the dining room. Arrangements of roses, pond lilies, magnolias, and ferns were four feet high or more. The room was bedecked with flags of many nations and huge tubs of pine trees surrounded by mosses and grasses. A boutonniere was placed at each plate.

Each guest received a menu card listing all the courses included in the dinner. For two hours, they feasted on Lynnhaven oysters on the half shell, two choices of soups, and a fish course consisting of sheepshead with hollandaise sauce, broiled bluefish, and baked trout with Italian sauce. Fillet of beef, saddle of mutton, spring chicken fried with cream, soft crabs on toast, lamb chops, prime ribs, and ham with champagne sauce were among the meat courses. Salads included chicken, crab, lobster, potato, and vegetable combinations.

There also were several varieties of potatoes, green peas, asparagus, and stewed and raw tomatoes. Desserts consisted of vanilla ice cream, lemon sherbet, champagne jelly, strawberries, and cheese, all accompanied by French coffee.

Black Sea Bass and Black Beans

Yield: 2 to 3 servings

1 2- to 3-pound sea bass or
   any firm-fleshed fish,
   cleaned with head on
3 tablespoons salted black
   beans (spiced) from a
   Chinese food store
2 tablespoons vegetable oil
1 teaspoon sugar
1 tablespoon pale dry sherry
2 tablespoons soy sauce
1 teaspoon ginger
1 garlic clove, chopped
3 to 4 spring onions,
   chopped with green part
   saved

Mix all ingredients except bass and green part of onion. Let stand 10 minutes. Rub mixture into fish and put rest in cavity of fish. Layer sliced green ends of onions on top of fish and in cavity. Place fish on a platter on a rack in a steamer with about ½ cup water in bottom and steam, covered, for about 20 minutes, depending on size of fish. It is important that the fish be on a platter when it is steamed so the marinade doesn't wash or drip off.

—Barbara Fine

Don Youngman's
Beer Batter for Bluefish

Yield: about 2 cups

1 beer
3 eggs, beaten
1½ cups self-rising flour
3 tablespoons baking
   powder
2 teaspoons salt
1 teaspoon lemon-pepper
Filleted bluefish, cut into
   small strips
½ cup vegetable oil

Combine first six ingredients. Dip fish into batter. Fry in oil, turning once when golden brown. Drain and serve.

—Bill Candler

Captain Seidman's Mock Crabcakes

Yield: about 12 cakes

2 cups boiled bluefish fillets
2 slices bread, broken up
1 tablespoon mayonnaise
1 tablespoon prepared
   mustard
1 tablespoon
   Worcestershire sauce
1 teaspoon Old Bay seafood
   seasoning
1 egg, beaten fluffy

Remove skin and dark meat from fish. Boil white meat until flaky. Mix all ingredients together and make patties. Fry them in hot oil until brown. This recipe should be doubled if you like crabcakes.

—Julie Ogden
Cookbook by Parents, Teachers, and Students of Creeds School, 1981

Broiled Bluefish

Large bluefish fillet, sliced
   into steaks
Seasoned cracker meal as
   needed
½ cup (1 stick) butter,
   approximately
Garlic salt to taste
Salt and pepper to taste

Preheat oven to 350 degrees F. Dredge bluefish steaks in cracker meal. Place in large flat baking dish with a little water. Sprinkle with garlic salt, salt, and pepper. Melt butter. Pour half the butter over the fillets. Bake about 20 minutes, depending on the size of steaks, until flesh is white and flaky. Remove from oven. Pour rest of butter on steaks. Sprinkle with more garlic salt, salt, and pepper. Run under broiler until top is brown and crispy.

—Janice Moore
Virginia Beach Seafood Company

Fried Catfish

Fried catfish is the popular Friday luncheon special at Mercer's Boathouse on the North Landing River. The Princess Anne Courthouse crowd makes a daily ritual out of lunch at "Vivian's," as the little restaurant is more affectionately known. Vivian Mercer and her cohort Polly Marshall make a point of using local fresh products whenever they can.

Yield: 3 to 4 servings

1 2- to 3-pound Blue
  Channel catfish, skinned,
  filleted, and cut into
  finger-size strips
1 cup cornmeal
1 cup pancake mix
1 teaspoon salt
1 teaspoon pepper
1 tablespoon seafood
  seasoning

Wash strips of catfish and while still wet, drench in mixture of meal, pancake mix, salt, pepper, and seafood seasoning. Drop strips into oil heated to 400 degrees F. and fry until golden brown.

—Vivian Mercer

Mercer's Boathouse on the North Landing River is a favorite luncheon spot for the Princess Anne Courthouse crowd. Illustration by Chris Nicholson

94

Duck-In Clam Chowder

In 1952 the Duck-In was a little roadside diner which was easy to "duck in" and get out in a hurry. The name stuck and today, though greatly expanded, the Duck-In remains a special landmark to Beach visitors crossing the Lesner Bridge on Shore Drive. Families with children, matrons out for lunch, watermen back from a morning's work, and businessmen all find the Duck-In to their liking. The rustic atmosphere, spectacular view, and good seafood combine to make it a favorite among locals and tourists alike. Duck-In Crabcakes and Clam Chowder are among the specialties.

Yield: 10 servings

½ pound bacon
20 large clams, chopped,
   with juice saved
1 pound onions, diced
2½ pounds potatoes, peeled
   and chopped
¾ cup flour

Fry bacon, crumble, and reserve grease. Fill large pot with 2 quarts of water. Add clam juice, onions, and bacon grease. Bring to a boil. Boil for 25 minutes. Add chopped potatoes. Cook until potatoes begin to soften. Add chopped clams and bacon. Continue to boil for 15 minutes. Thin flour slowly in 2 quarts of cold water, making sure to eliminate any lumps. Pour flour mixture slowly into pot, stirring as you pour. Boil for 5 to 10 minutes, stirring regularly. Serve hot in soup bowls.

—Bill Miller
The Duck-In

Beach Pub Clam Fritters

These fritters are a favorite accompaniment to the popular Sunday breakfasts at The Beach Pub on Laskin Road.

Yield: 10 fritters

1½ pounds chopped clams
2 eggs
1½ tablespoons Tabasco
  sauce
8 ounces flour
Salt to taste

Mix all ingredients. Fry in oil until golden brown. Turn and fry on other side until golden. Drain on paper towels.

—The Beach Pub

Pilot Boat Cod

For over 100 years, a pilot boat was anchored off Cape Henry, standing watch over the entrance to the Chesapeake Bay in much the same way the Cape Henry Lighthouse does. The boat, *The Virginia*, was a home away from home for Virginia Pilot Association pilots who guide visiting ships into the Hampton Roads harbor. When a ship approached the Chesapeake Bay channel, she was met by a pilot who was ferried from *The Virginia* in a small launch. *The Virginia* became known for her hearty seafaring meals, such as this robust breakfast, a favorite with the pilots and crews for many years. Today *The Virginia* has been retired and the pilots operate from a shore station near the Lesner Bridge over Lynnhaven Inlet.

Yield: 4 servings

1 one-pound box cod
3 to 4 pounds white
  potatoes
4 eggs, hard-cooked
1 cup chopped raw onions
1 pound bacon, cooked and
  drippings saved

Soak cod overnight, changing water often. Drain. Cook cod and potatoes in large pot of water, boiling gently about 20 minutes. When potatoes are done, so are the fish. Peel and chop eggs. Crumble bacon. Serve the potatoes and cod on a platter surrounded by small dishes of egg, onion, and bacon to be used as a garnish. Serve a pitcher of bacon drippings to pour over each serving.

—Bob Callis
Virginia Pilot Association

Clam Sauce with Spinach Noodles

Yield: 4 servings

4 tablespoons butter
5 tablespoons olive oil, divided
2 tablespoons finely chopped shallots or green onions
2 garlic cloves, crushed
2 tablespoons tomato paste
1½ cups clam juice
¼ teaspoon oregano
1 fresh tomato, chopped
1½ cups minced clams
2 tablespoons chopped parsley
1 pound spinach noodles
3 quarts water
2 tablespoons salt

To make the clam sauce, melt the butter with 4 tablespoons of the oil. Sauté the shallots and garlic for 2 minutes. Stir in the tomato paste. Add the clam juice and oregano and cook until half the liquid has boiled away. Add the chopped tomato, minced clams, and parsley. Keep warm until the pasta is ready.

To cook the spinach noodles, boil 3 quarts water and then add the salt, 1 tablespoon olive oil, and noodles. Cook until they are just short of being done, about 8 to 10 minutes. Drain, add the clam sauce, and serve.

—Peter Coe
Taste Unlimited

Deviled Clams

Alice Caffee is a member of the Virginia Beach Sand Witches. Established in 1964, the club is the first ladies fishing club in Virginia. Their cookbook is full of good recipes for seafood.

Yield: about 1 dozen clam shells

24 clams, removed from shell and chopped
Breadcrumbs as needed
½ cup clam juice
1 small onion, chopped fine
1 egg, beaten
½ cup tomato juice
1 teaspoon dried mustard
Pepper to taste

Preheat oven to 250 to 300 degrees F. Mix all ingredients using enough crumbs to make mixture stiff. Stuff sterilized clam shells with mixture. Sprinkle crumbs on top. Dot with butter and bake for 1 hour.

—Alice Caffee
Virginia Beach Sand Witches Cookbook,
1978

Steamed Crabs

In a large crab steamer or pot with rack on the bottom, add 1 cup vinegar and 1 cup water for a dozen live crabs. Between the layers of crabs, sprinkle 4 tablespoons seafood seasoning and 1½ tablespoons salt. Boil until crabs are red.

—Louisa Venable Kyle

How to Pick a Crab

1. With the cooked crab upside down, lift the small flap on the rear and pull it back and down. This should dislodge the top shell of the crab as well. If not, turn the crab over and lift the top shell by the pointed ends.
2. Remove the pincher claws and set them aside.
3. Remove the other legs by cutting them up close to the body.
4. On the upper side of the body, remove the gills and rinse out the intestines and spongy material.
5. Cut off the "face" of the crab. What is left is the "core" of the crab and contains all the white meat.
6. Cut off the upper two halves of the core by slicing from the inside toward the sides along the mid-line of the core. This will expose the lump meat found in the rear of the lower core section. Insert your knife under the lump and lift it out.
7. Remove the smaller pieces of white meat from the other pockets by running the knife in from where each leg was removed, then lifting up. Repeat this procedure with the upper section of core you removed in step 6.
8. Crack open the claws with your knife. Carefully remove the meat from within.

—Virginia Department of Agriculture and Consumer Services

Crabmeat Balls

Yield: 3 dozen medium-sized balls

3 tablespoons butter
3 tablespoons flour
1 cup milk
1 teaspoon salt
1/8 teaspoon pepper
3/4 teaspoon dry mustard
1/4 teaspoon Worcestershire
  sauce
1 tablespoon finely minced
  onion
2 cups crabmeat
Cracker crumbs as needed
2 eggs, beaten with a little
  milk

Make a cream sauce of butter, flour, and milk. Add salt, pepper, mustard, Worcestershire, and onion. Add crabmeat and mix. Chill. Drop from teaspoon into cracker crumbs and roll into ball. Dip first in eggs and then back into cracker crumbs. Place on cookie sheets to freeze and then store in bags. Deep fry in oil before serving.

—Shelby Webster

Crab Fingers

Yield: appetizers for 12

1 loaf sliced white bread
1 pound crabmeat
1/2 cup mayonnaise
2 tablespoons prepared
  mustard

Remove crusts from bread slices (save to make breadcrumbs). Toast only one side of bread; cut each slice into two or three fingers. Blend together crabmeat, mayonnaise, and mustard; spread untoasted side of each finger with crabmeat mixture. Broil until hot and bubbly.

—From "Made in Virginia" luncheon by the Culinary Arts Students at the Virginia Beach Campus of Tidewater Community College

Crab Melt-Aways

Yield: appetizers for 8

1 heaping tablespoon
   mayonnaise
4 to 5 ounces crabmeat
½ cup (1 stick) butter
1 5-ounce jar Cheddar
   cheese
Seafood seasoning to taste
16 toast rounds

Mix mayonnaise with crabmeat. Melt butter and cheese over low heat. Add to crabmeat mixture. Add seafood seasoning to taste. Pile mixture on toast rounds and broil until bubbly.

—Willa Engel

Crabmeat Salad

Yield: 3 cups

1 pound crabmeat
¾ cup chopped celery
2 tablespoons lemon juice
1 teaspoon salt
⅛ teaspoon pepper
3 tablespoons mayonnaise
1 teaspoon capers

Add all ingredients together and mix gently but thoroughly. Keep refrigerated until served.

—Hazel Sterling
Country Roads Cookbook
Tabernacle United Methodist Church, 1981

How to Fry Hard Crabs

You have to try this to believe it. When fried in this fashion much of the cartilage is edible.

Clean crabs. Remove back shell, legs, and claws. (Steam claws later.) With a tablespoon or the heel of your hand, gently crush the body of the crab to break the center membrane so that the crab will lie flat. Season crabs to taste with salt, pepper, seafood seasoning, and hot sauce. Roll in flour and fry in hot oil.

—Alice Caffee
Virginia Beach Sand Witches Cook Book, 1978

Crabcake Creation

This recipe is a long-time favorite at Tandom's Pine Tree Inn on Virginia Beach Boulevard at Lynnhaven. The inn began in 1922 as The Little Lynnhaven Inn, located in what is now the parking lot at the bottom of the hill. In 1927 the owners built the restaurant you see today and named it the Pine Tree Inn. For many years it was one of the few restaurants between the Beach and Norfolk. Its Sunday lunches were especially popular. In 1980 the restaurant became Tandom's Pine Tree Inn and still attracts those who love good food.

Yield: 8 servings

1½ pounds lump backfin
   crabmeat
½ cup mayonnaise
½ quart breadcrumbs
1 tablespoon
   Worcestershire sauce
1 tablespoon dry mustard
½ tablespoon salt
½ teaspoon white pepper
2 whole eggs
1½ tablespoons red wine
   vinegar
½ teaspoon Accent
Peanut oil for frying

Mix all ingredients together. Make into cakes. Finish off with breadcrumb coating. Fry in peanut oil until light golden brown.
—Tandom's Pine Tree Inn

Minnie's Stewed Crabs

This recipe is a North Carolinian way of cooking crabs, says Mac Rawls, who is the director of the Virginia Museum of Marine Science and quite a fisherman.

Yield: 4 servings

12 hard crabs, cleaned,
   broken in half with
   appendages removed,
   and scrubbed well
¼ cup bacon grease
1 quart water
1 tablespoon cornmeal to
   thicken juices
Salt and pepper to taste

Mix all ingredients except crabs in saucepan. Bring mixture to a boil, add crabs and appendages, and then cook very slowly for about 20 minutes. Serve with biscuits to sop up the stew.
—Mac Rawls

Duck-In Crabcakes

Yield: 10 servings

4 eggs
6 tablespoons mayonnaise
3 tablespoons mustard
1 tablespoon seafood
   seasoning
1 teaspoon Worcestershire
   sauce
4 ounces breadcrumbs
½ cup diced onions
2 pounds crabmeat

Hand mix all ingredients in a large mixing bowl. Form into 3½-ounce cakes, 1 inch in thickness. Fry in oil over medium heat until golden brown on each side.

—Bill Miller
The Duck-In

DUCK-IN
EST. 1952
VA. BEACH, VA.

The Duck-In, established in 1952, is a familiar landmark on the northeast side of the Lesner Bridge on Shore Drive. Illustration by Rick Fusco

Crab Mousse Hood

Yield: 1 5-cup mold

8 ounces cream cheese
1 10-ounce can cream of
  mushroom soup
1 cup finely chopped celery
1 medium onion, finely
  chopped
1 cup mayonnaise
1 6-ounce can crabmeat or
  ½ pound crabmeat
3 tablespoons unflavored
  gelatin, dissolved in
  ½ cup cold water
2 tablespoons lemon juice
2 tablespoons
  Worcestershire sauce
1 teaspoon minced garlic
Dash salt and pepper

Melt cream cheese and soup together. Mix celery, onion, mayonnaise, crabmeat, dissolved gelatin, lemon juice, Worcestershire sauce and garlic. Add to cream cheese mixture and blend well. Pour into mold. Chill at least 6 hours. Serve with crackers.

—Margaret Hood

Crab Mousse Robb

Virginia Governor Charles S. Robb and his family often vacation at the governor's cottage at Camp Pendleton, the Virginia National Guard headquarters in Virginia Beach. This crab mousse is one of the recipes Lynda Robb uses for summertime entertaining.

Yield: appetizers for 8

8 ounces crabmeat
1 cup mayonnaise
1 10-ounce can cream of
  mushroom soup
1 3-ounce package cream
  cheese
1 small onion, finely
  chopped
1 cup finely chopped celery
1 package unflavored
  gelatin, dissolved in
  3 tablespoons cold water

Mix crabmeat and mayonnaise. Heat mushroom soup and add cream cheese. Stir until cheese is melted. Add to crabmeat along with onion and celery. Add gelatin and pour into wet fish mold. Chill overnight.
Note: When unmolded, the fish may be decorated with pimiento, olive slices, and parsley. Serve with sesame seed crackers.

—Lynda Robb

Crab and Asparagus Soup

Yield: 4 servings

4 cups homemade chicken
    stock
1 egg
1 small can white
    asparagus, chopped
¼ pound crabmeat
1 tablespoon cornstarch
Salt and pepper to taste

Bring stock to a boil. Beat egg well and pour over stock, stirring constantly. Add cornstarch mixed with a little water to soup to thicken. Add asparagus, crab, salt, and pepper.

—La Caravelle

Crab Casserole Herbert

This casserole is a favorite at church suppers at Emanuel Episcopal Church in Kempsville. Established in 1843, the church was in the population center of early Princess Anne County. Emanuel was destroyed by fire in 1943; however, it was rebuilt in the same architectural style and at the same location. The altar cross, communion silver, and lectern are the originals from the first church.

Yield: 4 servings

1 pound crabmeat, picked
    over and shell removed
½ cup mayonnaise
1 teaspoon seasoned salt
1 teaspoon Worcestershire
    sauce
5 tablespoons sherry
Several drops Tabasco
½ cup Durkee's dressing
1 cup crushed cheese
    crackers

Preheat oven to 350 degrees F. Mix first seven ingredients. Place in casserole dish and top with crushed crackers. Bake until browned, about 15 to 20 minutes.

—Kathryn Herbert

Crab Casserole Spitzli

Yield: 4 servings

1 pound picked backfin
  crabmeat
⅔ cup mayonnaise
⅓ cup Durkee's dressing
1 teaspoon savory salt
Dash Worcestershire sauce
¼ cup cracker crumbs
¼ cup grated cheese

Mix all ingredients together and put in baking dish. Cover top with crumbs and cheese. Dot with butter. Bake 30 minutes.

—Rita Spitzli

She-Crab Soup

Yield: 10 servings

1 medium onion, chopped
1 pound white crabmeat
2 quarts plus 1 pint milk
½ cup (1 stick) butter,
  divided
Worcestershire sauce to
  taste
Salt and pepper to taste
1 tablespoon cornstarch to
  thicken
¼ pound crab roe, chopped
½ cup sherry wine (dry wine
  may be used)
Paprika for garnish

Sauté onion over low heat in half of the butter until soft, but not brown. Add the crabmeat and heat. Heat the milk in top of double boiler, but do not boil. Add the crabmeat mixture and the rest of the butter to hot milk. Season to taste with Worcestershire sauce and sprinkle with salt. Stir cornstarch into ½ cup cold milk. Pour into soup to thicken. Add crab roe and sherry wine. Stir together well. Sprinkle a little paprika on each serving. Serve piping hot.

Note: Sherry may be added just before serving.

—Daphne Young
*Cookbook by Parents, Teachers,
and Students of Creeds School, 1981*

Crab Quiche

Yield: 4 to 6 servings

½ cup mayonnaise
2 tablespoons flour
½ cup milk
2 eggs, beaten
1⅔ cups crabmeat, flaked
8 ounces Swiss cheese,
  finely diced
⅓ cup chopped onion
1 9-inch pie shell, unbaked

Preheat oven to 350 degrees F. Mix mayonnaise, flour, milk, and eggs until well blended. Stir in crabmeat, cheese, and onion. Pour mixture into pie shell and bake for 40 to 45 minutes.

—Reba S. McClanan

Deviled Crab Casserole

Yield: 4 servings

4 slices buttered toast, cut in
  cubes
½ cup hot water
1 pound flaked crabmeat
1 medium onion, grated
2 eggs, lightly beaten
1 tablespoon
  Worcestershire sauce
1 tablespoon ketchup
Salt and pepper to taste
About 2 tablespoons butter

Preheat oven to 350 degrees F. Place toast cubes in mixing bowl and soften with hot water. Stir in crabmeat, onion, eggs, Worcestershire sauce, and ketchup. Mix well using hands. This way you can check for any shell that may have been left in crabmeat. Season with salt and pepper. Pack into shells or casserole dish and dot with butter. Bake 30 minutes.

Note: This dish can be prepared in the morning and kept in refrigerator until ready to cook for lunch or dinner.

—Mrs. James G. Kellam

How to Deep-Fry Soft-Shell Crabs

According to Robert Herman, owner of the Lighthouse Restaurant, soft-shell crabs should be breaded right before they are cooked. Otherwise, they get soggy because they are so moist. "Our breading is the closest to nothing we can use," Herman says. "We use a really light flour, no egg, no milk, no breadcrumbs, and no seasoning. We also use a really, really light cooking oil since soft-shells have a tendency to absorb grease."

The Lighthouse uses a separate fryer for the crabs. The crabs are not submerged all the way, just deep enough for them to float. They are cooked for 2½ minutes on each side.

"You've got to watch the color," Herman says. "Let them get golden brown and take them out before the batter begins to separate from the crab.

"What you want is the crab," he adds. "They're expensive as the devil, a real delicacy. Why, I'd bring the live crab out if you'd eat it."

—Robert Herman
The Lighthouse Restaurant

How to Clean Soft-Shell Crabs

Clean the crab while still alive, either right before you cook it or right before you freeze it. Using a pair of scissors, cut out the mouth and eyes. Cut off the apron on the back. Lift up each corner of the shell on the back and cut out the lungs or "dead man" as it is called. Wash well.

Drum Chowder

Yield: 12 servings

½ pound salt pork, cut in small pieces
3 tablespoons flour
4 cups water
1 tablespoon salt
½ teaspoon pepper
3 onions, sliced
2 pounds white potatoes cut in 3-inch cubes
4 pounds drum fish, cut in 3-by-2-by-1-inch pieces

Fry salt pork in dutch oven or heavy pot. Remove when brown. Add flour to pork drippings and mix thoroughly. Stir in water. Add salt, pepper, onions, and potatoes. Cook about 20 minutes until potatoes are almost done. Add drum and cook another 20 minutes. If cornmeal dumplings are added, put them in the pot for the last 15 minutes.

—Alice Caffee
Virginia Beach Sand Witches Cook Book, 1978

Fred's Fish Fry

Using a Coleman stove outside on the deck in the summertime, Fred Lowe often entertains guests with a fish fry. His cornbread and Nancy Lowe's coleslaw round out this traditional meal.

Yield: 8 to 10 servings

The Fish
4 pounds flounder or trout
  fillets
Salt to taste
3 eggs
1½ cups milk
½ teaspoon pepper
2 cups plain cracker meal
Peanut or vegetable oil as
  needed

Wash fish thoroughly in cold water. Cut into chunks approximately 1½ to 2 inches long. Allow to dry on paper towels. Sprinkle lightly with salt (or salt substitute). Beat eggs, milk, and pepper until well mixed. Place cracker meal in large heavy-duty grocery bag. Dip each piece of fish in the egg mixture and drop immediately into the bag. Holding the top of the bag closed, shake thoroughly until all the fish is coated with meal, adding more meal if necessary. Place oil at least ½-inch deep in large skillet, preferably cast iron. Heat until oil is very hot. Place enough fish in pan to permit easy turning. (Do not let fillets touch.) Reduce heat to medium high. Cook until golden brown on one side (2 to 3 minutes). Turn fish and repeat high-to-medium heat combination. (This high-medium heat ensures that the fish will not absorb the oil and will be crispy on the outside and flaky on the inside.) Remove and drain on paper towels.

Cornbread

2 cups regular cornmeal
1 teaspoon onion powder
1 tablespoon sugar
½ teaspoon salt
1 egg
About 1 cup milk
Peanut or vegetable oil as
  needed

Mix dry ingredients. Add milk and well-beaten egg. Mix well. Mixture should be the consistency of applesauce. Adjust accordingly with more meal or milk. Pour oil in cast iron skillet until it is ¼-inch deep and heat to medium high. Place a tablespoon of the mixture in the hot oil. Fry until golden brown on one side and turn and brown the other side. Do not overload the pan or allow pieces of cornbread to stick together. Drain on paper towel. Bread should be very crispy.

Nancy's Coleslaw

1 medium cabbage,
  shredded
½ to 1 small onion, grated
1 to 1½ cups mayonnaise
1 tablespoon celery seed
½ teaspoon sugar
1 tablespoon vinegar
Salt and pepper to taste

Combine cabbage and onion. Make dressing of remaining ingredients and toss cabbage and dressing.

—Fred Lowe

Flounder Casserole with Zucchini

Yield: 6 servings

½ dozen medium-sized
  fillets of flounder
1 medium onion, chopped
2 cups tomato sauce
1 whole, fresh zucchini, cut
  into thin slices (1 cup)
2 garlic cloves, finely
  chopped
1 green pepper, seeded and
  chopped
⅔ cup diced carrot
Grated Parmesan cheese to
  taste

Preheat oven to 350 degrees F. Place flounder in baking dish approximately 9-by-13 inches. Sprinkle with onion. Distribute tomato sauce evenly. Add sliced zucchini to cover. Add garlic, carrot, and pepper. Top with grated Parmesan cheese to taste. Bake approximately 30 minutes; sauce should be slightly bubbly. Serve with brown rice and green salad.

Note: Perch, sole, or any other firm-fleshed fish may be used.

—Anne Bérubé

Mussels à la Huguenot

Most people think of fresh mussels as purely a French dish, but mussels are readily available for the gathering in Tidewater. Check around the pilings of the Chesapeake Bay Bridge-Tunnel for one place. Paula Opheim, former Lynnhaven House administrator, can imagine this dish as something the eighteenth-century residents (who were Huguenot immigrants) of the house would enjoy.

Yield: 4 servings

½ cup (1 stick) butter
4 large onions, chopped fine
3 or 4 dozen small black
    mussels, scrubbed with
    beards removed
1 large bunch fresh parsley,
    chopped fine
1 pint fresh heavy cream

Melt butter in large enamel pan. Sauté onions and parsley in butter. Add mussels and pour in cream. Cook covered over low heat until shells pop open. Serve at once with crusty day-old French bread for dipping in the cream sauce and a salad and white wine. (Scoop up the butter and cream with an open mussel shell.)

—Paula Opheim
Former Lynnhaven House Administrator

Lynnhaven Oysters

The Lynnhaven oyster established itself firmly in the settlers' hearts early on. According to George Percy's recollection of the 1607 landing, a band of colonists explored the land around the Lynnhaven River and came upon a band of Indians roasting oysters around a campfire.

"They fled away to the mountains [sand dunes] and left many of the oysters in the fire," Percy wrote. "We ate some of the oysters which were large and delicate in taste."

He added later in his diary that "upon this plot of ground are a good store of mussels and oysters which lay on the ground as thick as stones." Also while exploring, the settlers bartered with the Indians for smoked oysters, which they had never tried before.

The Lynnhavens reached their peak of popularity in the late 1800s and early 1900s. Local oystermen still talk about the shipper who sent a barrel of Lynnhaven oysters to the King of England every Christmas. Internationally-famous turn-of-the-century gourmand Diamond Jim Brady always requested Lynnhaven oysters in his huge repasts. He would often eat, as an appetizer, two or three dozen oysters at least six inches long. Brady's affinity for Lynnhavens was well known among the shippers. One went so far as to send in every second or third shipment to New York a barrel of extra-large Lynnhavens with the words "For Mr. Brady" printed on the side.

At that time, Lynnhaven oysters were the *piece de resistance* at the Waldorf Astoria's oyster bar. And other restaurants of any consequence across the country listed not just "oysters," but "Lynnhaven oysters," on their menus.

Some say it's the salty sweet taste which sets Lynnhavens apart from other oysters. Whatever the difference, oyster lovers can always tell a Lynnhaven. Lynnhavens also are appreciated for their size. Most oysters come in the standard or select sizes. Lynnhavens also come in a size known as "counts," great big ones for eating raw.

Today the Lynnhaven oyster is becoming a thing of the past. The Lynnhaven River is often closed to oystering because of pollution. Whenever Virginia Beach residents get a yearning for a Lynnhaven, however, they can reminisce about the time President William Howard Taft visited O'Keefe's Casino, an oyster house at Cape Henry, in 1909.

O'Keefe's served the president a true Princess Anne County feast of Lynnhaven oysters on the half shell, bowls of roasted Lynnhavens, and platters of Princess Anne turkey and Smithfield ham. Standing on a chair, the president made an impromptu talk after the meal was over.

"Gentlemen, I feel like an oyster and I ought to be as dumb as one, but when you get on the soil of old Virginia, there is something about it that makes you feel like talking . . ." the local paper quoted him as saying.

After giving the highest praises to the Lynnhavens—"the best oysters with the finest flavor"—he went on to say what the group of maritime businessmen was waiting anxiously to hear.

"We ought to put a gigantic fortress right here between these capes," he said, sweeping his arm out toward the area which became Fort Story.

Everyone knew the Lynnhaven oyster had a powerful effect on the palate, but no one dreamed it could have such an impact on national defense!

Buying Oysters

- The best oysters are "unwashed" and generally can be found only where the shucking is done on the premises.
- Seaside oysters are those taken from the ocean side of the Eastern Shore rather than the Chesapeake Bay side. They are apt to be more salty than bayside oysters.
- "Select" oysters are bigger oysters, not better oysters. "Selects" are best for frying while "Standards" are good for stewing.
- Oysters are good eating year around. The old rule of thumb that oysters are only good in the "R" months probably was created in the days when summer refrigeration was not dependable.

Chesapeake Oysters and Smithfield Ham en Brochette

Yield: 10 servings

30 fresh oysters, shucked
30 4-by-4-inch paper-thin slices Smithfield, Westphalian, or Black Forest ham (about 7½ ounces)

Preheat indoor grill or prepare outdoor barbecue. Wrap each oyster tightly in one slice of ham and secure each with bamboo skewer. Grill until charred, about 5 minutes; turn once.

—Recipe by Peter Coe first appeared in *Bon Appetit®* magazine

Oyster Stew Page Davis

Yield: 4 servings

1 large onion, chopped
1 tablespoon butter
1 quart "cream line" milk
¼ cup kuzu arrowroot (this
   is a product the Japanese
   make of the kudzu vine—
   high in calcium)
½ cup chopped fresh
   parsley
1 bay leaf
1 pint oysters
Butter, salt, and pepper to
   taste

Sauté onions in butter. Add milk and kuzu. Stir until kuzu is dissolved (about 10 minutes). Add parsley and bay leaf. Simmer until thick (about 10 minutes). Add oysters and simmer another 10 minutes. Add salt, pepper, and butter. Serve.

—Page Davis

How to Shuck an Oyster

Wash and rinse the oysters thoroughly in cold water. Open, or shuck, the oyster by placing it on a table, flat shell up, and holding it with the left hand. With the right hand, force an oyster knife between the shells at or near the thin end. To make it easier to insert the knife, the thin end, or "bill," may be broken off with a hammer—a method preferred by most cooks. Now cut the large adductor muscle close to the flat upper shell in which it is attached and remove the shell. Cut the lower end of the same muscle which is attached to the deep half of the shell and leave the oyster loose in the shell if it is to be served on the half shell, or drop it into a container. After shucking, examine the oysters for bits of shell, paying particular attention to the muscle, to which pieces of shell sometimes adhere.

—Virginia Seafood Council

Fondue Pot Oysters

When you want to serve raw or roasted oysters but don't want to fool with the shells, try this as a substitute. Melt a stick of butter in a fondue pot. Add a dash of Worcestershire sauce and a pint of unwashed oysters with liquor. Heat until edges just curl. Keep warm over a flame and serve with cocktail sauce on small plates with oyster forks. This comes very close to the panned oysters found at oyster roasts.

—Mary Reid Barrow

Creamed Oysters on Smithfield Ham

For many years, until he moved to the Eastern Shore, the Reverend Joe Pinder tended an oyster bed as well as his flock at All Saints Episcopal Church on Great Neck Road. This is one of his favorite oyster recipes.

Yield: 6 to 8 servings

½ cup (1 stick) butter
1 pint oysters, unwashed if possible
5 tablespoons flour
2 cups milk
¼ pound Smithfield ham, thinly sliced
Cornbread, corn cakes, toasted English muffin halves or toast

Melt butter in skillet. Add oysters with liquor. (If there is not much liquor, add a cup of salted water.) Heat oysters in pan until edges begin to curl. Quickly remove oysters from pan and set aside. (Oysters will toughen and shrink if cooked too long.) Blend flour and milk in blender. Add mixture to oyster liquor and bring to a boil, stirring constantly. Remove from stove and return oysters to sauce. Place slices of ham on top of bread. Ladle oysters and sauce on top of ham and serve with vegetables of your choice.

Note: The ham is used for flavor, not as filler. Oysters and ham complement one another. Creamed oysters may be served over rice without the ham, but it is not quite as tasty as with ham.

—The Reverend Joe Pinder

Oyster Stew
Virginia Beach Seafood Company

Yield: 6 to 8 servings

1 quart standard oysters, cut
  in half
3 tablespoons oyster liquor
1 quart milk
½ cup (1 stick) butter
Salt and pepper to taste

Place oysters, liquor, milk, and butter in saucepan and beat over medium heat until oysters float to the top. Add salt and pepper to taste. Cook 10 to 15 minutes over medium-low heat.

—Richard and Janice Galloway, Owners
Virgina Beach Seafood Company

Caffee-Style Oysters

Yield: 4 servings

1 pint oysters with liquor
2 tablespoons butter
3 teaspoons lemon juice
Worcestershire sauce to
  taste
Thin slices of Cheddar or
  Swiss cheese, cut to fit
  oyster

Preheat oven to 350 degrees F. Place oysters with juice in flat baking dish large enough so that the oysters aren't layered. Dot with butter and sprinkle with lemon juice and Worcestershire sauce, to taste. Bake until edges begin to wrinkle, about 10 minutes. Remove oysters from oven and set oven temperature on broil. Put a piece of cheese on top of each oyster and broil until the cheese is bubbly.

—Alice Caffee

Creamed Oysters with Virginia Ham

Yield: 6 servings or 12 appetizers

1 quart fresh shucked
   oysters
1 pound fully cooked
   Virginia ham
½ cup (1 stick) melted
   butter or margarine
¼ cup flour
2 cups heavy cream
1 cup reserved oyster liquor
½ cup milk
¼ cup sherry
½ teaspoon salt
¼ teaspoon pepper

Drain liquor from oysters into a bowl and set aside. Cut ham into ½-inch cubes. Combine butter and flour together until smooth; cook over medium heat until mixture turns a light yellow. Gradually stir in cream, oyster liquor, milk, sherry, salt, and pepper. Cook over medium heat, stirring constantly 8 to 10 miutes. Add oysters and ham cubes; cook an additional 5 minutes. Pour mixture into a chafing dish; keep warm over a low burner. Serve over toast points.

—Virginia Seafood Council

Oysters Easter Lynnhaven House

Former Lynnhaven House Administrator Paula Opheim has devised a modern-day version of oysters Rockefeller. She says to open two dozen fresh Chesapeake Bay oysters and roast in a 300 degree F. oven on a bed of rock salt for about 20 minutes. While oysters are roasting, chop three small onions very fine in a food processor with ½ cup white wine. In microwave cook one package of frozen spinach soufflé for 4 minutes. Stir in onions and wine. Cook 2 minutes. Stir and cook 4 minutes more. Put a dollop of spinach soufflé on top of each oyster and serve.

—Paula Opheim
Former Lynnhaven House Administrator

Oysters in Mornay Sauce

Yield: 8 servings

4 dozen oysters
3 tablespoons ketchup
6 tablespoons chili sauce
Juice of ½ lemon
2 to 3 tablespoons
   horseradish
3 to 4 drops Tabasco
2 tablespoons butter
2 tablespoons flour
1 cup milk
¼ cup grated Swiss cheese
1½ tablespoons grated
   Parmesan cheese
¼ teaspoon salt
White pepper to taste

Preheat oven to 450 degrees F. The oysters may be prepared individually in clean shells or arranged in a big flat baking dish. Make a seafood sauce with ketchup, chili sauce, lemon juice, horseradish, and Tabasco. Put a dollop on each oyster. Melt butter in saucepan, add flour, and mix well. Slowly add milk, stirring constantly over low heat until thickened. Remove from heat. Add cheeses and seasonings and blend well. Cover seafood sauce and oysters with the Mornay sauce. Run into a hot oven until oyster edges begin to curl and sauce is light brown.

—Michelene Mower

Oyster Patties

Yield: 8 large patties

2 large eggs
1 cup self-rising flour
3 tablespoons vegetable oil,
   divided
Pepper to taste
1 pint shucked standard
   oysters with liquor
4 tablespoons butter or
   margarine

Beat eggs, Add flour, 1 tablespoon oil, and pepper. Stir in oysters and liquor. Heat butter and 2 tablespoons oil in large skillet. Add oysters and batter to skillet like hotcakes. Fry over moderate heat until brown on both sides.

—Mary Reid Barrow

Oyster Pie Rappahannock

Yield: 1 9-inch pie

1 pint standard oysters,
    fresh or frozen
6 slices bacon
2 cups sliced fresh
    mushrooms
½ cup chopped onion
½ cup chopped green onion
1¾ cups flour, divided
½ teaspoon salt
¼ teaspoon cayenne pepper
¼ cup chopped parsley
2 tablespoons lemon juice
1 tablespoon butter or
    margarine, at room
    temperature
2¼ teaspoons baking
    powder
¼ teaspoon salt
3 tablespoons butter or
    margarine
½ cup milk

Thaw oysters if frozen. Drain oysters; dry between absorbent paper. In a 10-inch skillet cook bacon until crisp. Remove bacon; drain and crumble. Reserve 3 tablespoons bacon fat. Add mushrooms, onion, and green onion to reserved bacon fat. Cover and simmer 5 minutes or until tender. Blend in ¼ cup flour, salt, and pepper. Stir in oysters, bacon, parsley, and lemon juice. Grease a 9-inch pie plate. Turn oyster mixture into pie plate.

Preheat oven to 400 degrees F.

Sift dry ingredients together. Cut in butter until mixture is like coarse crumbs. Add milk all at once. Mix just to a soft dough. Turn onto lightly floured surface. Knead gently five to six strokes. Shape into a ball. Roll out to a 9-inch circle to fit on top of pie plate. Cover oysters with biscuit topping. Score biscuit topping to make a design on top. Bake at 400 degrees F. for 20 to 25 minutes or until biscuit topping is lightly browned. Cut into wedges. Makes six servings.

—Virginia Department of Agriculture
and Consumer Services

Scalloped Oysters McClanan

Yield: 4 servings

½ pound saltine crackers,
    crumbled
1 pint standard oysters
½ cup (1 stick) butter
Salt and pepper to taste
4 cups milk, approximately

Preheat oven to 350 degrees F. Place a layer of crackers in a greased 2-quart casserole dish. Add a layer of oysters. Sprinkle with salt and pepper. Dot with butter. Make another layer of crackers, oysters, salt, pepper, and butter. Pour milk over all. Bake for 35 to 40 minutes or until puffed and lightly browned.

—Reba S. McClanan

Oysters and Sweetbreads

Louisa Venable Kyle has been writing about local history and lore for many years. Many of her recipes were included in "A Country Woman's Scrapbook" which was published in *The Virginian-Pilot* for six-and-a-half years. Some of these recipes also can be found in a collection of her columns by that same name.

Yield: 6 servings

1 pound sweetbreads
6 tablespoons flour
6 tablespoons butter
1 teaspoon salt
Dash red pepper
3½ cups milk
Dash Worcestershire sauce
½ cup finely chopped celery
2 tablespoons chopped
    parsley
1 pint oysters
2 egg yolks, beaten
2 packages pie crust mix,
    mixed according to
    package directions

Preheat oven to 425 degrees F. Prepare sweetbreads by soaking in cold water 1 hour. Plunge in boiling water and cook 10 minutes; drain and place in cold water until chilled. Remove membrane. Cook oysters in saucepan with liquor just until edges curl. Drain, saving ½ cup liquor. Make cream sauce by melting butter in a saucepan. Add flour, salt, and red pepper. When blended, add milk and Worcestershire sauce and cook until thick. Add celery and parsley. Add ½ cup oyster liquor and egg yolks to sauce, stirring constantly until thickened again. Roll pie crust thin. Line the bottom and sides of a 2-quart casserole with pastry, saving enough to cover top of casserole. Cut up sweetbreads and add to cream sauce. Add oysters and pour mixture into casserole lined with pastry. Cover with extra piece of pastry. Bake until crust is golden brown, about 20 minutes.

—Louisa Venable Kyle

Scalloped Oysters Evans

Irvin Evans, a Lynnhaven oysterman, says he can always tell a Lynnhaven oyster from other oysters by its taste. "It's just like eating chalk and cheese," he says. "You can tell the difference." This recipe is Mrs. Evans' favorite. For many years, it was a highlight of the Scott Memorial United Methodist Church holiday bazaar.

Yield: 12 servings

1 quart shucked oysters
2½ cups saltine crackers, broken up coarsely
1 16-ounce can good quality corn or same amount of fresh corn, cut from cob
¾ cup (1½ sticks) butter

Preheat oven to 375 degrees F. Drain oysters and reserve liquor. Grease a 9-by-13-inch casserole with butter. Place a layer of crackers on the bottom. Add a layer of oysters and a thin layer of corn. Dot with butter. Repeat each layer and end up with cracker crumbs. Spoon about one-third of the oyster liquor over the crumbs and slice butter evenly over the casserole. Bake for about 45 minutes or until it firms up.

—Mrs. Irvin Evans

Oyster-Mushroom Stuffing

Yield: 9 cups of stuffing

1 pint oysters
1 pound mushrooms, coarsely chopped
1½ cups chopped celery with leaves
1 cup chopped onion
½ cup (1 stick) butter or margarine
2 cups soft breadcrumbs
¼ cup chopped parsley
2 tablespoons diced pimiento
2 teaspoons salt
1½ teaspoons poultry seasoning
¼ teaspoon black pepper
2 eggs, beaten

Check oysters for any shell particles. Drain oysters, reserving liquor. In a 10-inch skillet, sauté mushrooms, celery, and onion in butter until tender but not brown. Combine breadcrumbs, parsley, pimiento, and seasonings. Add oysters, oyster liquor, vegetables, and eggs to breadcrumbs. Mix thoroughly. To serve as a side dish place stuffing mixture in a well-greased 2-quart casserole. Bake at 350 degrees F. for 25 to 30 minutes.

—Virginia Seafood Council

Oyster Stuffing

Yield: stuffing for small turkey

1 pint oysters
8 slices bread
1 heaping tablespoon
   melted butter
1 teaspoon sugar
Salt to taste

Cut oysters into small pieces, saving the oyster liquor. Soak bread in warm water, squeezing out the water. Add to oysters and liquor. Add the butter, sugar, and salt. Mix thoroughly.

—Effie Munden

Oyster Crabs

Real oyster aficionados say the tiny pale pink crab, found living in the oyster shell and which often ends up in containers of unwashed oysters, is a real delicacy. If enough are available, oyster lovers will eat the little crabs, deep fried or sauteed. Others pop them into their mouths, just as they would an oyster, and swear they are delicious.

Virginia Beach. Watercolor by H. Moser, 1889. Courtesy of the Virginia State Library

Coquille St. James

Yield: 4 servings

5 to 8 tablespoons butter
2 tablespoons minced onion
¼ pound fresh mushrooms,
  quartered
¾ to 1 pound bay scallops
2 tablespoons dry white
  wine
1 egg yolk
2 tablespoons milk
3 tablespoons flour
1 cup milk
4 tablespoons grated mild
  white cheese
4 tablespoons grated
  Parmesan cheese
Cayenne pepper to taste
1 tablespoon chopped
  parsley

Preheat broiler. Sauté the onion until tender in 3 to 5 tablespoons butter. Add mushrooms and scallops and more butter if necessary to coat mushrooms and scallops. Add wine and simmer 10 minutes. Drain liquid. Beat 1 egg yolk with 2 tablespoons milk. Melt 3 tablespoons butter. Add flour to make a roux. Add remaining milk, stirring constantly. When sauce begins to thicken, add 2 tablespoons of sauce to egg. Pour egg mixture into saucepan, stirring constantly. Add 2 tablespoons each of the white and Parmesan cheeses. Stir until melted. Add scallop mixture to sauce. Add dash of cayenne and parsley. Fill four au gratin dishes. Top with rest of white and Parmesan cheeses. Run under broiler until bubbly and brown.

—Caroline Kennett

Shad

The coming of the shad on their annual migration into the bay and up the rivers to spawn heralds the coming of spring in Virginia Beach. From the time the colonists arrived, shad has been considered a delicacy and an important commercial fish. The sweet delicate flesh and the myriad of bones, however, make the consumption of shad an agony and an ecstasy. For those who want to cook a shad whole, rather than filleted, the traditional way is to bake it in a tightly covered pan at 300 degrees F. for 5 hours or more. This slow-baking method will leave the large backbone soft enough to eat and most of the little bones will have dissolved.

Others swear that planking is the only way to cook shad. From the time of George Washington, shad plankings have been an excuse for politicians to gather for a day of eating, drinking, and good companionship. The annual shad planking in nearby Wakefield, Virginia, has become a traditional spring ritual for most Virginia politicians. Some say the Indians taught the early settlers how to plank shad. Others say the Philadelphia Fish House Eating Club invented the technique, which is nothing more than cooking shad on an oiled plank of wood over an open fire.

A Canadian Indian legend blames the shad's many bones on its former life as a discontented porcupine. The porcupine asked the Great Spirit to give it a new existence, the legend says. The spirit grabbed the porcupine, turned it inside out, and threw it in the river to begin life anew as a shad.

And now every spring, Virginia seafood lovers praise the Great Spirit for giving them shad.

How to Bone a Shad

Scale the shad and cut fillets from either side. With the fillet flesh side up, feel with your fingers for the three ridges of bone which run the length of the fillet. With a sharp knife, slice the flesh paralleling and close to each side of the three rows of bones, taking care not to slice through the skin. After slicing, tear each strip of flesh away from the skin. The bones come too and you have a boneless shad fillet with three wedges of flesh missing.

Boneless Shad In A Brown Bag

This recipe and Shad Roe and Egg Scramble belonged to Helen Wise's mother, Mrs. James Edwin Smith. Mrs. Wise remembers the shad dinners from her childhood in Princess Anne County, first at Oceana and then in Birdneck Point.

Yield: 6 servings

3 or 4 pounds shad
2 quarts water
2 tablespoons vinegar
1 small onion, chopped
2 tablespoons butter
Salt and pepper to taste
4 strips bacon
1 large square cheesecloth
1 large brown paper bag,
　well greased with
　vegetable oil

Preheat oven to 250 degrees F. Place cleaned shad in large piece of cheesecloth with chopped onion. Lower it into gently boiling water to which vinegar has been added. Boil for 20 minutes.

Take shad out by lifting cheesecloth. Cover shad inside and out with butter and seasonings. Cover with bacon strips. Place shad in the paper bag and then in a roaster. Cover and cook for 6 hours. The bones will dissolve.

—Helen Wise

Ice House Shad

Milton Warren's Ice House Restaurant on Norfolk Avenue is indeed an ice house which was built around 1900 to serve the commercial fishermen. Later it served the hotels and residences in old Virginia Beach. It was renovated into a restaurant in 1975 and is especially noted for the fresh local produce and seafood on its menu.

Yield: 1 serving

8 to 10 ounces shad fillet
Lemon juice to taste
Butter to taste
White pepper, salt, and
　paprika to taste

Preheat oven to 350 degrees F. Place shad in a broiler pan with a little water. Sprinkle with lemon juice; dot with butter. Season with pepper and a touch of salt. Bake for about 20 minutes. Do not turn it. When flesh has firmed up, add more butter, sprinkle with paprika, and run under broiler until golden.

—Milton Warren

124

Planked Shad

Get a nice fat shad, very fresh. (The gills of a fresh fish are red, not purple.) Put the plank in the oven to get very hot. Split the shad, lay it open flat, and wipe it dry. Lay it skin side down on the hot plank, sprinkle with salt and pepper, and bake in moderately hot oven till done. Butter the shad generously before sending it to the table. Garnish with lemon and parsley: a wreath of the parsley, and wedges of the lemon at intervals. Or have a rim of mashed potatoes. Have ready the mashed potatoes and when the dish is nearly ready to serve take it out and press the potatoes through a pastry tube in any form you like. Then use a few sprigs of parsley and lemon. You can of course make the dish as elaborate as you like by adding tomatoes, cucumbers, and other vegetables around the fish. But be sure the fish is served as soon as done, very hot.

—Mary D. Pretlow's
The Calendar of Old Southern Recipes
Courtesy of Kirn Memorial Library

Shad Roe

The roe of the female shad is a true delicacy and is considered by many to be far better than the shad itself. Lightly floured, sauteed gently in butter, and served with new potatoes and asparagus, shad roe is the epitome of a spring meal.

Shad Roe with Asparagus

Peter Coe, owner of the Taste Unlimited stores in Tidewater, is a very fine cook as is his wife Susan. Their menu of Tidewater Virginia foods was featured in the May 1983 issue of *Bon Appétit.*

Yield: 10 servings

5 pairs shad roe
10 teaspoons butter
10 teaspoons dry white wine
10 teaspoons fresh lemon
  juice
2½ teaspoons chopped
  fresh tarragon
Salt and freshly ground
  pepper to taste
½ cup (1 stick) melted
  butter
Juice of 1 medium lemon
30 asparagus spears (about
  1½ pounds), stalks
  snapped at natural
  breaking point
Vegetable oil for frying
10 lemon wedges for
  garnish

Separate each pair of roe into halves. Center one half on right side of 12-by-12-inch square of waxed paper. Dot with 1 teaspoon butter and drizzle with 1 teaspoon wine and 1 teaspoon lemon juice. Sprinkle with ¼ teaspoon tarragon. Season with salt and pepper. Fold paper over and roll up edges to seal. Repeat with remaining halves. (Can be prepared up to 2 hours ahead to this point.) Blend melted butter and lemon juice. Cook asparagus in large pot of boiling salted water until crisp-tender.

Meanwhile, pour oil into large skillet to depth of ¼ inch. Heat oil over medium heat. Add roe packages in batches and cook until paper is browned, about 4 minutes on each side. Keep roe warm in packages in preheated oven set at lowest temperature. Drain asparagus and pat dry. Unwrap roe and transfer to individual heated plates. Arrange three asparagus stalks on side of each roe. Drizzle asparagus with lemon butter. Garnish with lemon wedges and serve.

—Recipe by Peter Coe
first appeared in *Bon Appétit®* Magazine

Shad Roe and Egg Scramble

Yield: 2 to 3 servings

1 set shad roe
4 eggs
1 teaspoon butter or bacon
grease
Salt and pepper to taste

Melt fat and brown shad roe lightly. Break roe and pour in beaten eggs. Scramble together as for scrambled eggs. Season.

Note: A 1-pound can of herring roe, drained, may be substituted for shad roe.

—Helen Wise

Hilltop Seafood Barbecue

Peel and devein jumbo shrimp. Wrap each in one-half strip of bacon. Secure with a toothpick. Lay wrapped shrimp in broiler pan. Surround with barbecue sauce. Broil until bacon is just crisp, about 6 minutes. Turn shrimp over and broil for 6 more minutes.

—Donnie Sanderson
Hilltop Seafood

Champion Shrimp Baste

The Champion Horseradish Company has been making horseradish products in Norfolk since 1925. Sharon Lathrop and her husband Lyle, who live in Virginia Beach, work in the family business.

Yield: 2 servings

½ pound peeled, deveined
shrimp
2 tablespoons Champion
Horsey mustard
3 shakes Worcestershire
sauce
1 capful white wine

Mix ingredients well. Brush with pastry brush over each shrimp. Broil until done, turning shrimp once and brushing other side.

—Sharon Lathrop

127

Shrimp, D & M Marina Style

The D & M Marina on the Lynnhaven Inlet has operated charter fishing boats and a fresh seafood shop for the past nineteen years.

Yield: 4 servings

4 quarts cold water
½ jar mustard
2 pounds shrimp

Add mustard to cold water in large pot. Stir. Add shrimp. Bring to a boil. Remove from heat and drain shrimp. The mustard doesn't alter the flavor of the shrimp but does keep them tender and juicy.

—Katie Davis
D & M Marina

Shrimp Casserole

Yield: 4 servings

1 10-ounce can cream of
   mushroom soup
1 small onion, chopped
1 tablespoon melted butter
1 tablespoon lemon juice
1 package long-grain and
   wild rice mix, cooked
   ahead of time according
   to package directions
1 teaspoon Worcestershire
   sauce
1 teaspoon dry mustard
½ teaspoon pepper
¾ cup shredded mozzarella
   cheese
1½ pounds cleaned shrimp,
   uncooked

Preheat oven to 350 degrees F. Mix ingredients in the order listed. Pour into greased 2-quart casserole. Bake 45 minutes. Check to make sure shrimp are done. This recipe is elegant and simple.

—Susan Kolodny

Shrimp and Scallops with Rice

Yield: 5 servings

1½ green peppers, sliced
1 pint basket pearl onions,
   skins removed
½ pound fresh mushrooms,
   quartered
½ cup (1 stick) butter
½ pound bay scallops
1 pound shrimp, cooked
   and shelled
¾ cup dry sherry
1 teaspoon lemon juice
1 teaspoon thyme
Dash Worcestershire sauce
Salt and pepper to taste
3 medium tomatoes,
   skinned and cut into
   eighths, or 1 15–ounce
   can, drained and chopped
1 package long-grain and
   wild rice mixture, cooked
   according to package
   directions

Sauté peppers and onions in half of the butter until soft. Add mushrooms and sauté quickly. Save vegetables. Melt the remaining butter and sauté the scallops and shrimp. Add sherry and seasonings. Add pepper, onions, tomatoes, and mushrooms and simmer gently for about 30 minutes. Serve over long-grain and wild rice mixture.

—Mary Reid Barrow

Shrimp Tempura

Yield: 8 servings

3 pounds large, cleaned,
   raw shrimp, split down
   the middle and scored
Salt to taste
2 cups flour
2 cups cold water
½ teaspoon baking powder
1 egg, beaten
Salt and pepper to taste

Salt shrimp. Mix a batter of flour, water, baking powder, egg, salt, and pepper. Dip shrimp in batter. Deep fry in oil. Vegetables can be deep fried in this batter also.

—Rita Spitzli

Shrimp Scampi

Yield: 4 servings

1½ sticks unsalted butter
¼ cup finely chopped onion
3 to 4 crushed garlic cloves
4 chopped parsley sprigs
1 pound uncooked,
    deveined medium shrimp
¼ cup dry white wine
2 tablespoons lemon juice
Salt to taste
Freshly ground pepper to
    taste

Melt butter in medium skillet over low heat. Sauté onion, garlic, and parsley about 10 minutes. Add shrimp and stir until pink. Remove shrimp and keep warm. Add wine and lemon juice to skillet; simmer 2 to 3 minutes. Season to taste with salt and pepper. Pour over shrimp.

—Bob Callis
Loaves and Fishes, III
Galilee Episcopal Church, 1982

Baked Fish

This recipe of Janie Dudley's is typical of the fare eaten by the brave "surfmen" who manned the Seatack Lifesaving Station at 24th Street and Atlantic Avenue when Roy Dudley was in charge. The first Seatack station was built in 1879 when Congress established the U.S. Lifesaving Service and authorized four lifesaving stations at Virginia Beach. The present station, now the Virginia Beach Maritime Historical Museum, was built in 1903. Memorabilia from such tragic incidents as the wreck of the Norwegian bark *Diktator* are housed in the renovated old station.

Yield: 6 servings

1 4- to 5-pound trout,
    cleaned
Salt, pepper, and flour as
    needed
1 tablespoon butter
5 to 6 white potatoes, peeled
    and sliced
3 to 4 onions, peeled and
    sliced
3 slices bacon
1 cup water

Preheat oven to 400 degrees F. Place fish in greased pan and salt and pepper well. Sift a little flour over the fish. Dot with butter. Place potatoes and onions around the fish and salt and pepper them well. Lay bacon on top of fish. Add about 1 cup water to pan, but do not let water cover the fish. Bake, covered, until potatoes are tender. Remove lid and allow fish to brown.

—Janie Dudley

The Old Coast Guard Station

The old Coast Guard Station is now the Virginia Beach Maritime Historical Museum, located at 24th Street and Atlantic Avenue. Courtesy of the Virginia Beach Bank of Commerce

Seaside Sandwich

Yield: 4 sandwiches

2 cups shrimp, cooked and
   peeled
2 cups grated Cheddar
   cheese
1 teaspoon dillweed
1 cup sliced ripe olives
1 cup mayonnaise
2 mini-French loaves,
   halved and buttered
1 avocado, sliced

Mix shrimp, cheese, dillweed, olives, and mayonnaise. Spread mixture on bread. Top with sliced avocado and place under broiler until bubbly.

—Betty Ann Huger

Trout Almondine

Mary Lynn Perney is a member of the Virginia Beach Anglers Club and writes a column, "Favorites from the Galley," for the club newsletter *Tight Lines.* The Virginia Beach Anglers Club was formed in 1959 when local members of the Tidewater Anglers Club decided they wanted a club of their own. The large group is well known throughout the state as a top fishing club and is also active in conservation efforts.

Yield: 6 servings

2 pounds trout fillets
¼ cup flour
1 teaspoon salt
1 teaspoon paprika
4 tablespoons melted butter
½ cup sliced almonds
2 tablespoons lemon juice
4 drops hot pepper sauce
1 tablespoon chopped
   parsley

Cut fillets into six portions. Combine flour, salt, and paprika. Roll fish in mixture and place skin-side down in a greased baking dish. Drizzle 2 tablespoons melted butter over top. Broil 4 inches from heat source for 10 to 15 minutes or until fish flakes easily. While broiling, sauté almonds in remaining butter until golden brown, stirring constantly. Remove from heat and add lemon juice, pepper sauce, and parsley. Pour over fish and serve.

—Mary Lynn Perney
Virginia Beach Anglers Club

Striped Bass

As far back as colonial times, the striped bass was known as the "boldest, bravest, and most active fish" that visited the rivers and bays along the Atlantic coast.

Along with cod, the bass ranked as one of the most important fisheries in the New World. As early as 1639, the colonists saw fit to protect the bass with the first conservation measures ever enacted in America. The laws forbade the use of the fish as fertilizer.

Today, bass, known locally by many as rockfish, still is very popular with both sport and commercial fishermen. It is a rare treat, however, when Virginia Beach fishermen bring home striped bass. These fish must swim upstream to spawn in brackish or fresh water, and river pollution and dams which block the passageways up the rivers have combined to destroy much of the breeding habitat.

Today, the fish is the subject of a great number of studies in hopes of reversing this trend. The white flaky flesh is of the highest quality.

Rockfish Wahab
(Striped Bass)

Yield: 6 to 8 servings

8 to 12 pounds rockfish (or any other fish) scaled and cleaned
4 strips bacon
1 to 2 large cans tomatoes
6 to 8 potatoes, peeled
6 to 8 carrots, scraped
6 to 8 medium onions, skinned
1 to 2 cups white wine or water
Salt to taste
Pepper to taste
Oregano to taste
Parsley to taste

Preheat oven to 325 degrees F. Soak fish in salted ice water for 30 minutes. Score fish on one side and lay on greased baking rack in pan. Place bacon across scoring and pour wine or water, tomatoes, and seasonings over fish. Place vegetables around fish, making sure they are in liquid. Cover pan with foil. Bake, basting every 30 minutes, for 1½ to 2 hours. Remove foil last 30 minutes. Broil a few minutes if bacon is not browned. Garnish with parsley.
—Betty Wahab

Stuffed Rockfish

(Striped Bass)

Yield: 6 servings

¼ cup chopped onions
3 tablespoons chopped
    green onion
4 tablespoons butter
1 3-ounce can chopped
    mushrooms, drained and
    liquid reserved
About 7 ounces crab meat
½ cup coarse saltine
    cracker crumbs
½ teaspoon salt
¼ teaspoon pepper
3 pounds dressed rockfish

Sauce
3 tablespoons butter
3 tablespoons flour
¼ teaspoon salt
Milk as needed
⅓ cup dry white wine
4 ounces (1 cup) grated
    Swiss cheese
½ teaspoon paprika

Preheat oven to 400 degrees F. Sauté onion in butter in skillet until tender but not brown. Stir in drained mushrooms, crab-meat, cracker crumbs, salt, and pepper. Place mixture inside fish and spread left-overs on top of fish.

To make sauce, melt 3 tablespoons butter in saucepan. Blend in flour and salt. Add enough milk to reserved mushroom liquid to make 1½ cups and add with wine to saucepan, stirring constantly. Cook until thickened and bubbly. Pour over fish. Bake for 25 minutes. Sprinkle with cheese and paprika. Return to oven. Bake 10 minutes longer.

—Willa Engel

Grilled Tuna

Yield: 4 servings

8 tuna fillets, 1 inch thick
Soy sauce to taste
Salt and pepper to taste
Mayonnaise as needed

Lay fillets on heavy-duty foil. Sprinkle with soy sauce, salt, and pepper. Coat the top of each fillet with a thick layer of mayonnaise. Wrap in foil and cook on grill 10 to 15 minutes or until meat is white and flaky. Fillets also can be baked at 350 degrees F. for 15 minutes or until done.

—Donnie Sanderson
Hilltop Seafood

Tuna (or Shrimp) Lasagna

Add fresh tuna or shrimp, instead of ground beef, to your favorite lasagna recipe for an unusual twist to an old stand-by.

—Donnie Sanderson
Hilltop Seafood

Fresh Tuna Salad

Yield: 3 to 4 servings

1 pound fresh tuna steak
1 onion, chopped
2 stalks celery, chopped
¾ cup mayonnaise
Juice of ½ lemon
Freshly ground pepper to taste
Dash garlic powder

Soak tuna in water overnight in refrigerator. The next day, simmer until done (depending on thickness of steak) about 20 to 30 minutes. Cool. Crumble into flakes in bowl. Mix in remaining ingredients.

—Mary Reid Barrow

Meat

Princess Anne County: A Fine Place for Livestock

In 1728 William Byrd, II was one of a group of Virginians and North Carolinians who surveyed the boundary line between the two states. He kept a diary of the trip in which he described Knotts Island as a fine place to raise livestock, that the sheep were as large as those in England. He wrote, however, that the residents paid for their fine sheep and cattle by "losing as much blood in the summer season by the infinite number of mosquetas as all their beef and pork can recruit in the winter."

The Pavilion, the city's new convention center, is named after the Pavilion at the first Virginia Beach Hotel. Courtesy of the Virginia Beach Bank of Commerce

Pavilion Canapes

The Virginia Beach Pavilion opened its doors in the spring of 1981. The new structure is designed to serve the growing convention trade at the Beach. It also houses a fine theater for cultural productions. The early Pavilion was a seaside one, built in 1883 adjoining the first hotel in Virginia Beach. The following canapes are a favorite cocktail food at post-theater parties at Pavilion. Catered by Servomation, Pavilion food ranges from simple barbecue to elegant full-course meals.

Roast Beef Pickles

Spread a thin slice of roast beef with room-temperature cream cheese. Lay a slice of dill pickle in the center of the roast beef and roll up. Stick enough toothpicks (4 to 5) into roll to divide it into bite-size pieces, then slice. Arrange canapes with toothpicks on serving dish.

Ham Roll-Ups

Follow the same procedure for Roast Beef Pickles, except substitute country ham for the roast beef and canned or fresh cooked asparagus for the pickle.

—Stephen Latham, Chef
Virginia Beach Pavilion

Abigail Thelaball Boeuf Bourguinon

Paula Opheim, former Lynnhaven House administrator, named this recipe in honor of the wife of Francis Thelaball, builder of the Lynnhaven House. She uses the fresh rosemary in the Lynnhaven House herb garden and wild onions from the yard, just as Abigail would have done.

Yield: 6 servings

4 tablespoons butter
2 garlic cloves, peeled and crushed
2½ to 3 pounds round beef steak, cut into large pieces
Flour as needed
5 medium onions, peeled and quartered
1 pound fresh mushrooms, whole if small, or sliced if large
2 cans beef gravy
1 beef gravy can of red burgundy wine
1 sprig of fresh rosemary and a clump of wild spring onion tops, snipped with kitchen shears

Melt butter in large dutch oven. Add garlic. Salt, pepper, and dredge meat in flour. Brown the meat in butter and then pour off all but 3 tablespoons of the drippings. Add onions, mushrooms, beef gravy, wine, rosemary, and spring onion shoots. Simmer about 3 hours. Serve over egg noodles or rice or just dip French bread into it.

—Paula Opheim
Former Lynnhaven House Administrator

Mary Champe's Spiced Beef

This spiced beef should be started three weeks before the Christmas holiday. The recipe may be cut in half if a ten-pound roast is too large.

Yield: 10-pound spiced beef

1 10-pound round steak
   roast, rolled and tied
1 pint salt
1 pint black molasses
3 ounces saltpeter (from
   drugstore)
2 ounces nutmeg
2 ounces allspice
2 ounces cloves

Mix salt, molasses, saltpeter, nutmeg, allspice, and cloves. Pat into beef. Place in large crock with any remaining mixture. Cover with a plate. Turn every three days for three weeks. Cook by slowly boiling in water to cover, 20 minutes to the pound. During the holidays, serve sliced thin much the same way you would serve Smithfield ham.

—Mary Reid Barrow

Beef Stick

Yield: 3 rolls

2 pounds regular
   hamburger
3 level tablespoons *curing*
   salt
½ teaspoon garlic salt
½ teaspoon onon salt
½ teaspoon black pepper
¼ teaspoon marjoram
¼ teaspoon ground sage
1 teaspoon sugar
½ teaspoon celery seed
1 cup water

Mix all ingredients well with hands. Refrigerate 1 hour to set. Divide into three logs or rolls. Roll tightly in aluminum foil and tie with string in three places. Refrigerate for three days to cure. After three days, preheat oven to 350 degrees F. and put rolls in a cake pan with 1 inch of water. Bake in oven for 1 hour and 15 minutes, turning several times. When cool, unwrap and rewrap in clean foil. Keep refrigerated. Slice beef stick and serve with favorite cheese and crackers. Will keep approximately two weeks after cooking.

Note: You must use curing salt.

—Judy Humphries

Beef Stroganoff

Yield: 4 to 6 servings

2 pounds beef fillet, cut in
   half-inch slices
4 slices bacon
1 cup minced onion
½ pound mushrooms, sliced
1 10½-ounce can beef
   bouillon
1 8-ounce can tomato sauce
   (optional)
1 teaspoon salt
1 teaspoon Worcestershire
   sauce
¼ teaspoon rosemary
¼ cup dry white wine
1 cup sour cream
Wild rice for 6 people

Cut beef slices into half-inch strips. Fry bacon until crisp. Remove from pan. Brown beef in bacon drippings. Remove from pan. Cook onion and mushrooms in drippings until tender and lightly browned. Add bouillon, tomato sauce (if desired), salt, and Worcestershire sauce. Return beef to pan. Simmer 15 minutes. Add sour cream. Stir well. Serve on top of rice with a dollop of sour cream and parsley as a garnish.

—Betty Michelson

Marinade for Beef

Yield: 1 cup

⅓ cup vinegar
⅓ cup vegetable oil
3 tablespoons brown sugar
3 tablespoons soy sauce
2 medium onions (white or
   red)
1 garlic clove, minced
½ teaspoon pepper

Combine all ingredients. Marinate beef for desired length of time, depending on cut. Remove meat and cook. Heat remaining onions and liquid and serve with the beef.

—Susan Kolodny

Dining at the Life Saving Station

"Capt. De Lon, the Keeper, and his family greeted me cordially and at noon, ushered me out to the Station dining room to as good a dinner on fresh fish, just out of the sea, and fried chicken, just out of the fattening coop, as a weary traveler ever got at Jimmie Jones's in Norfolk." —concerning a visit to the False Cape Lifesaving Station in 1912, as recorded by the Reverend D. Gregory Claiborne Butts in *From Saddle to City by Buggy, Boat and Railway,* published in 1922.

Chicken Curry Balls

Yield: 3 dozen

¼ pound cream cheese, at room temperature
2 tablespoons mayonnaise
1 cup chopped cooked chicken
1 tablespoon curry powder
1 tablespoon chopped chutney
½ teaspoon salt
1 cup blanched slivered almonds
½ cup grated coconut

Mash cream cheese. Add mayonnaise, chicken, curry, chutney, salt, and almonds. Mix well and roll into walnut-size balls. Roll in coconut. Chill. They may be prepared a day in advance. This recipe freezes well.

—Elice Little
VF-101, Oceana Naval Air Station
A Flight Plan Before Dinner, 1982

Barbecued Chicken Wings

Yield: appetizers for 12

3 pounds chicken wings
½ cup soy sauce
½ cup barbecue sauce
¼ cup dry white wine
¼ cup vegetable oil
3 tablespoons sugar
2 garlic cloves
Ginger to taste

Marinate chicken in remaining ingredients for 16 hours. Preheat oven to 325 degrees F. and bake for 1 hour.
—Norma Dunn

Parmesan Baked Chicken Wings

Yield: 24 appetizers

2 cups finely grated
    breadcrumbs
¾ cup grated Parmesan
    cheese
¼ cup minced fresh parsley
2 teaspoons salt
½ teaspoon pepper
¼ teaspoon red pepper
    flakes
1 garlic clove, minced
24 chicken wings
2 sticks unsalted butter,
    melted and cooled

Preheat oven to 350 degrees F. Combine first seven ingredients. Remove tips from wings; halve the wings. Dip in melted butter and coat with crumb mixture. Arrange in pan and spoon on remaining butter. Bake 30 to 40 minutes, basting.
—Mary Crabbs
CTWL, Oceana Naval Air Station
A Flight Plan Before Dinner, 1982

Chicken Salad

Yield: 8 servings

1 whole chicken or white
   meat may be used, finely
   cut
Stalk of celery, finely cut
Mayonnaise as needed
Salt to taste

Cook chicken in water until well done. Remove and cool; then separate bones and skin from meat. Cut meat medium fine with knife (do not grind). Wash and cut celery medium fine, having equal parts of celery and chicken. Mix with enough mayonnaise until the mixture is good and moist. Season with salt to taste.

—Melva Riggs
Country Roads Cookbook
Tabernacle United Methodist Church, 1981

Firehouse Sweet and Sour Chicken

Jack Fremeau of the Virginia Beach Fire Department is known as the best firehouse cook in the city. This is a favorite of the men at the Princess Anne Plaza fire station.

Yield: 4 servings

1 3-pound chicken, cut up
⅓ cup flour
1 teaspoon salt
¼ teaspoon red pepper
⅓ cup vegetable oil
1 cup sugar
2 tablespoons cornstarch
¾ cup cider vinegar
1 tablespoon soy sauce
½ teaspoon ginger
1 chicken bouillon cube
1 13½-ounce can pineapple
   chunks, drained with
   liquid reserved
1 large green pepper, cut
   into strips

Preheat oven to 350 degrees F. Wash and dry chicken. Coat with flour seasoned with salt and red pepper. Fry chicken in oil until lightly browned. Place chicken in shallow baking pan, skin side up. In a saucepan, combine sugar, cornstarch, vinegar, soy sauce, ginger, bouillon cube, and pineapple liquid with enough water added to liquid to make 1¼ cups. Bring to a boil, stirring constantly. Cook for 2 minutes. Pour over chicken and bake 30 minutes. Add pineapple chunks and green pepper and bake 30 more minutes. Serve over white rice.

—Jack Fremeau

Eastern Shore Chapel
Chicken and Wild Rice Casserole

This is a popular item at the church bazaar's Chilly Gourmet Shop.

Yield: 12 servings

2 3-pound fryers
1 cup water
1 cup dry sherry
½ teaspoon curry
½ cup sliced celery
1½ teaspoons salt
1 medium onion, sliced
12 ounces long-grain and
 wild rice mix
Chicken broth plus enough
 water for cooking rice
1 cup sour cream
1 10½-ounce can
 condensed cream of
 mushroom soup
1 pound fresh mushrooms,
 sliced and sautéed in
 ¼ cup margarine

Place first seven ingredients in a deep kettle. Simmer 1 hour. Take chicken out and refrigerate. Strain broth. Cut cooled chicken in small pieces. Preheat oven to 350 degrees F. Cook rice in broth and water. Combine rice, chicken, sour cream, soup, and mushrooms. Pour into 9-by-13-inch pan. Bake 1 hour.

—Chilly Gourmet Shop
Women of Eastern Shore Chapel
Episcopal Church

Cavalier Hotel
Breast of Chicken Jerusalem

The luxurious Cavalier Hotel at 42nd Street and Atlantic Avenue was built as a community project to promote the growth of Virginia Beach. It opened its doors in 1927. The 250-acre facility included a golf course and a beach club. In the 1970s the new Cavalier Hotel was built on the oceanfront and the old hotel was restored to its original elegance. This recipe is a favorite of diners at the new Cavalier's rooftop dining room, Orion's Roof.

Yield: 5 servings

5 boneless chicken breasts
Flour as needed
Salt and pepper to taste
4 tablespoons butter
20 mushrooms, sliced
15 canned artichokes, cut in
   half

Veloute Sauce
2 sticks margarine
½ cup flour
2 cups milk
2 bouillon cubes
Salt and pepper to taste
¼ cup champagne
¼ cup vermouth
Breadcrumbs as needed
Parmesan cheese to taste
Butter as needed

Dredge chicken breasts in flour seasoned to taste with salt and pepper. Sauté in butter about 10 minutes or until browned on both sides. Set chicken aside. Sauté mushrooms and artichokes. Set aside. Preheat oven to 400 degrees F. To make veloute sauce, melt margarine in saucepan. Add flour and stir to make a smooth roux. Add bouillon cubes and add milk gradually, stirring constantly to make a thick, smooth sauce. Add champagne, vermouth, and salt and pepper to taste. Line bottom of individual casserole dishes with sauce. Cut breasts into about five large chunks each and place over sauce. Add mushrooms and artichokes, divided evenly among breasts. Cover with sauce. Top with breadcrumbs, Parmesan cheese, and dots of butter. Bake about 20 minutes until brown and bubbly.

—David Cherry, Chef
The Cavalier Hotel

The Cavalier Hotel

The Cavalier Hotel was built in 1927. Courtesy of the Virginia Beach Bank of Commerce

Chicken with Raisins and Almonds

Yield: 2 servings

Roasting chicken (whole or
    split in halves)
Ground herb mix,
    consisting of cardamom,
    black pepper, coriander,
    cloves, and ginger
¼ cup minced onions
2 tablespoons butter
¼ cup raisins
¼ cup slivered almonds
Heavy cream as needed
Yogurt as needed

Remove skin from chicken; massage and coat with ground herb mix; let sit for 30 minutes. Preheat oven to 350 degrees F.

Brown onions in butter, adding raisins and almonds. Blend and add equal parts cream and yogurt to desired basting consistency. Roast chicken for time consistent with size and weight. Baste frequently with raisin-almond sauce.

—Joe Lyle

Supreme de Volaille à la Diable

Yield: 8 servings

2 cups fresh breadcrumbs
1 cup grated Parmesan
    cheese
1 tablespoon salt
½ cup chopped, fresh
    parsley
1½ cups (3 sticks) butter
2 garlic cloves, crushed
1½ tablespoons good
    mustard
1½ teaspoons
    Worcestershire sauce
Monterey Jack cheese for
    stuffing (use Swiss or
    Muenster if not available)
8 boned chicken breasts
8 lemon wedges

Preheat oven to 350 degrees F. Combine in a bowl the breadcrumbs, Parmesan cheese, salt, and parsley. Melt butter and combine with garlic, mustard, and Worcestershire sauce. Take 8 scoops of Monterey Jack with a melon ball scooper and place a scoop on each breast. Fold the breast over the cheese, securing with string or toothpicks. Dip each cheese-stuffed breast first in butter mixture, and then in crumbs. Place on baking sheet lined with foil. Drizzle any butter that is left over the top of each breast. Bake about 1 hour. Remove string or toothpicks and serve each breast with a lemon wedge.

—Michelene Mower

Joe Pinder's Brunswick Stew

This brunswick stew, made by the Reverend Joe Pinder, is a favorite with the crowd at the annual Eighteenth Century Fair presented by the Princess Anne Historical Society at Upper Wolfsnare, a handsome Georgian structure built in 1759 by Thomas Walke. At one time the home was part of a 7,000-acre working plantation. The house was saved from annihilation by Virginia Beach Expressway construction in 1966 and turned over to the Historical Society which has had it renovated. The society opens Upper Wolfsnare to the public several times a year.

Yield: 60 to 70 gallons

140 pounds fryers
30 to 40 pounds beef, cubed, gristle and fat removed
15 pounds bacon
12 #10 cans tomatoes
12 #10 cans diced white potatoes
12 #10 cans lima or butter beans
6 #10 cans white corn
3 #10 cans okra
5 pounds dehydrated onions

Using large cast iron pots over a wood fire, cover the chickens with water and boil until they are coming apart. Remove from pots and pick, returning only edible meat to the pots. (Save giblets for other dishes.) Add beef to chicken and broth and return to slow boil. Add vegetables in equal portions to cooking pots. Pots have to be stirred continuously to prevent scorching. Once pots are brought to a boil, the fire can be decreased in order to maintain a slow boil. This needs to be maintained for several hours, stirring regularly until the meats and vegetables begin to come apart. Dice bacon and cook in skillet until crisp. Add bacon with grease in equal portions to cooking pots. Stir. Season with salt, black pepper, and red papper (with a cautious hand). Serve with cornbread, hush puppies, sweet potato biscuits, or breadsticks. It's a meal, not an appetizer!

—The Reverend Joe Pinder

Stir-Fried Chicken and Vegetables

Yield: 6 servings

2 to 2½ pounds chicken breasts, skinned, boned, and cut into thin strips
1 teaspoon paprika
2 tablespoons hot vegetable oil
1 large onion, thinly sliced
1 to 2 large green peppers, cut into thin strips
¾ cup celery, sliced diagonally
1 can water chestnuts, sliced
1 cup fresh mushrooms, sliced or whole
1 to 1½ cups fresh broccoli flowerets or Chinese pea pods
1¼ cups chicken broth, divided
2 tablespoons cornstarch
3 tablespoons soy sauce
Hot cooked rice for 6

Season chicken with paprika. Sauté in hot oil about 2 to 3 minutes. Add onion, peppers, celery, chestnuts, mushrooms, and/or broccoli, and/or Chinese pea pods along with ½ cup chicken broth. Cover and cook about 1½ minutes. Combine ¾ cup chicken broth, cornstarch, and soy sauce. Mix well. Add to skillet, stirring well. Cook about 1 to 2 minutes or until sauce thickens. Serve over hot rice.

—Susan Kolodny

Houston Sandwich

Yield: 4 sandwiches

2 whole chicken breasts
Vermouth as needed
2 mini-French loaves, halved and spread with mayonnaise
1 grapefruit, sectioned
1 ripe avocado, thinly sliced
4 slices Monterey Jack cheese

Steam chicken breasts in a little water and vermouth until tender. Cool. Skin and bone. Layer bread with hunks of chicken, grapefruit, and avocado. Top with cheese. Broil until bubbly.

—Mary Jane Willis

Roast Lamb Café

Yield: 8 servings

1 6- to 7-pound leg of lamb
Salt, pepper, and garlic
   powder to taste
Prepared mustard as
   needed
½ cup light brown sugar
1 cup strong coffee
½ cup white wine
⅛ teaspoon garlic powder

Preheat oven to 300 degrees F. Place lamb in shallow roasting pan. Season well with salt, pepper, and garlic powder. Smear lamb all over topside and underneath with mustard. Pat brown sugar, enough to cover mustard, on top of the lamb. Try to keep sugar from falling to bottom of pan. Pour coffee into the bottom of the pan. Place lamb in oven and begin to baste only after it has roasted for 45 minutes. (This gives the mustard-sugar coating a chance to get brown and crusty.) Make sure bottom of the pan is constantly covered with coffee or falling sugar will burn. Then baste every 15 minutes. Cook for about 2 hours for rare roast. When roast is done, remove it and set on a warm platter. Keep warm. Set pan itself over direct heat on top of range and let juices bubble up. Add wine and garlic powder and let it boil and bubble, using a wire whisk to get all the juice and crust up. Serve as gravy with the roast.

—Suzanne S. Jacobson

How to Cook a Smithfield Ham

1. Soak the ham in cool, clear water for 12 hours, or longer if desired. Those objecting to a salty taste should soak the ham for 24 hours, changing the water at the halfway point.
2. Wash the ham thoroughly, using a stiff brush, removing all mold and pepper.
3. Place ham in a deep pot (preferably oblong) skin down, and cover with cool water. Bring water to 180 degrees F. (not quite simmering), then cook for about 25 minutes per pound. Add water to keep ham covered.
4. When done, lift ham from the pot and remove skin and fat (as desired) while still warm.
5. If a sweet coating is desired, score ham and cover with brown sugar and place in an oven at 400 degrees F. for 15 minutes.

Warning: Do not cut the ham before cooking, but cook whole. This keeps the juice in.

—Gwaltney of Smithfield

How to Cook a Country Ham or a Smithfield Ham

1 country ham or 1 Smithfield ham*

Wash and scrub ham thoroughly. Put ham on stove in lard tin or container large enough to completely cover ham with COLD water. Bring to a boil without lid, or put lid partly on pot. Boil 1 minute per pound. Seal with lid. Set on board padded thickly with newspapers (1 to 1½ inches thick) opened wide. Bring newspapers up around container and tape snugly. Cover top with same amount of newspapers, bring down, and tape snugly. Throw rug or quilt (something heavy) over container. Let stand 24 hours. Take ham out of container and PLEASE BE CAREFUL because water is very, very hot.

Trim fat from ham. Now ham is ready to slice and serve plain or to serve your favorite way.

*If using Smithfield ham, cover with water and soak overnight before cooking. Pour off soaking water. Cover ham with cold water and continue as instructed above.

—Mrs. H. Finley Hatch

Pork With Distinction

Will Rogers once said that Virginia was famous for three products: rattlesnakes, presidents, and razorbacks.

Virginia Beach may not have contributed much to the reputation in the way of rattlesnakes and presidents, but the city can take a lot of credit for the razorbacks. Virginia Beach until just recently was the largest hog producing county in the state, a result of an industry begun in colonial times.

In those days, the animals led a contented life, roaming freely in the woods foraging on acorns and other wild foodstuffs, much like their wild boar cousins in Europe. Relatives of these early pigs occasionally can be seen living wild in the Back Bay—False Cape area.

By 1745 hogs were driving the citizens of Newtown in Princess Anne County wild. That year, the General Assembly passed a law which forbade hogs at large in Newtown. If any hogs were found running loose, it would be lawful to kill them.

"A great number of hogs are raised and suffered to go at large...to the great prejudice of the inhabitants thereof," the law explained.

Despite the troubles caused by free-roaming hogs, it wasn't until a century later with the arrival of the agricultural revolution that most hogs were confined and raised in a systematic fashion. Malbon Brothers Farm, established in 1923, is the father of modern hog production in Virginia Beach.

Virginia Beach hogs go to Smithfield, Virginia, to be slaughtered and inevitably some of these hogs end up as Smithfield hams. There is a certain distinction in ending up as a Smithfield ham, rather than just any old ham. It is said that during the early part of this century the royal family in England insisted upon a Smithfield ham and Lynnhaven oysters for Christmas dinner.

How to Slice a Virginia Ham

The most delightful flavor of Virginia ham can be enjoyed from very thin slices. Thus, a very sharp knife, preferably long and narrow, is needed.

First, with the ham on a platter, dressed side up, make a cut perpendicular to the bone about six inches in from the end of the hock. Cut a wedge-shaped piece from the ham so as to leave the cut surface at an angle of 45 degrees. Then start slicing very thin slices at an angle of 45 degrees, bringing the knife to the bone.

As the slices become larger, you should decrease the angle of the knife to obtain approximately equal servings. Eventually, the bone structure will make it necessary for you to cut smaller slices at different angles to the bone.

—Virginia Department of Agriculture and Consumer Services

Howard Gwaltney's
Favorite Smithfield Ham Casserole

Preheat oven to 350 degrees F. Cut off a few large slices of cooked ham and place on the bottom of a casserole. Cover with about 1 inch of cooked crabmeat. Add a top layer of ham slices, and place in oven for about 20 minutes or until the juices from the ham mix thoroughly with the crabmeat. Serve hot.

—Gwaltney of Smithfield

156

An Old-Fashioned
Princess Anne County Christmas

Years ago, a Princess Anne County family did not need to be wealthy to celebrate the holiday with a table rich with homegrown sweet potatoes, collards, and other vegetables. Princess Anne turkeys, home-cured hams, and chickens were plentiful as were wild game and oysters. Black walnut trees also grew wild and so did cranberries in the bogs near the North Landing River.

Almost anyone could have a Christmas tree, too. One had hardly to step outside the door to find a Virginia cedar tree to cut and bring in the house which would then be filled with the aroma of fresh-cut cedar. Strung with popcorn and wild rosehip garlands and hung with tulip poplar seed pods and gum balls, it was a poor man's tree fit for a king.

Ham and Crab Sandwich

Yield: 4 sandwiches

2 English muffins, halved
   and spread with
   mayonnaise
4 pieces Smithfield ham or
   Canadian bacon
4 tablespoons crabmeat
2 cans artichoke hearts
1 onion, minced
1 tomato, sliced
1¾ cups mayonnaise
1½ cups grated sharp
   cheese

Preheat oven to 350 degrees F. Layer bread with ham or bacon, crabmeat, sliced artichoke hearts, and 1 slice tomato. Mix mayonnaise and cheese and "ice" each sandwich with mixture. Bake 15 minutes.
—Mary Jane Willis

Dining at "Woodland"

"Woodland" was a farm in what is now the Baycliff neighborhood of the Beach. Anna, Alice, and Fanny Overstreet were sisters who grew up at Woodland. Anna was the great-grandmother of Betty Michelson, a Virginia Beach lawyer, who has a collection of letters exchanged by the sisters and their father and mother in the 1870s. Food is often mentioned, such as the time Alice wrote her sister Fanny that she had "been oystering and caught some of the largest fellows you most ever saw."

Letters also mention dinners of suckling pig "brown as a berry," stewed apples, coconut pies, suet dumplings, ham, baked chicken, "dewberries and milk," quarter of lamb shoulder, and Irish potatoes "grown on the farm."

Princess Anne County life may have been simple, but the food was fit for the most elegant table.

Stuffed Pork Chops

Yield: 6 servings

6 ¾-inch thick rib pork
   chops
1½ cups breadcrumbs
¼ cup chopped celery
¼ cup chopped onion
2 tablespoons chopped
   parsley
½ teaspoon salt
½ teaspoon pepper
Milk to moisten
1 cup rich milk or cream

Preheat oven to 350 degrees F. Either you or your butcher cut the bone from the meat and trim off excess fat. Cut a 1½ inch slit into the side of the chop, slipping knife inside to cut pocket. Wipe off chops with damp cloth and sprinkle with salt and pepper on the outside of chop. Fill pockets with stuffing of breadcrumbs, celery, onion, parsley, and seasonings moistened with milk. Sew in place with coarse thread and needle; tie. Sear chops in hot skillet and place in oven-proof glass casserole. Pour the cup of rich milk or cream over chops. Cover and bake chops 45 minutes to 1 hour. Thicken gravy with flour; use additional milk if more creamy gravy is desired.

—Edna Malbone
What's Cooking at Charity
Charity United Methodist Church, 1962

Cold Marinated Pork Loin

This is delicious at a large spring or summer buffet, served with Curried Rice Salad.

Yield: 12 servings

1 5- to 6-pound pork loin roast, tied, with fat cut out
Dried mustard as needed
Thyme as needed
½ cup sherry
½ cup soy sauce
2 garlic cloves, chopped
1 inch fresh gingeroot, sliced
1 8-ounce jar currant jelly
1 tablespoon soy sauce
2 tablespoons sherry

Rub roast with mustard and thyme. Mix sherry, soy sauce, garlic, and gingeroot in pan or bowl large enough to hold roast. Marinate the roast in the mixture overnight. Preheat oven to 325 degrees F. Cook roast, basting occasionally with sherry mixture for about 3 hours or until pork is no longer pink inside. Cool. Melt jelly. Add soy sauce and sherry. Cook, stirring until thickened. Pour glaze over pork and chill until ready to serve. Slice thin.

—Shelby Balderson

Barbecued Pork Chops

Reba McClanan, a member of Virginia Beach City Council, calls this the way to barbecue pork chops "the simple, forgetful way."

Yield: 4 servings

1 cup ketchup
1 cup coffee (teaspoon instant coffee dissolved in 1 cup water)
1 tablespoon Worcestershire sauce
¼ cup sugar, or less
½ cup vinegar
Salt and pepper
8 pork chops

Preheat oven to 300 degrees F. Mix first six ingredients in large baking dish. Add raw pork chops. Bake uncovered from 2 to 2½ hours. Baste with sauce occasionally.

—Reba S. McClanan

California Pork Chops

Yield: 6 servings

6 loin or rib pork chops,
  1 inch thick
Salt and pepper to taste
¼ cup flour
Vegetable oil as needed
2 oranges, peeled and sliced
5 tablespoons brown sugar,
  divided
2 teaspoons cornstarch
½ cup wine, chicken stock,
  or water
1 cup orange juice
½ teaspoon dried marjoram
3 medium onions, sliced
2 tablespoons parsley

Preheat oven to 350 degrees F. Trim excess fat from chops and fry fat out in skillet. Discard scraps when brown. Season chops with salt and pepper. Dredge in flour. Brown well in hot fat, adding a little oil if there is not enough fat from pork trimmings. Arrange the browned chops in one layer in a large, shallow casserole. Sprinkle orange slices with 3 tablespoons brown sugar. Set aside. Combine cornstarch, wine, orange juice, marjoram, and remaining brown sugar. Pour mixture over chops. Arrange onions on top and sprinkle with parsley. Bake 1 hour. Arrange orange slices on top and bake 15 minutes more.

—Caroline Kennett

Shanghai Pork Chops

Yield: 2 servings

2 pork chops
1 tablespoon vegetable oil
1 onion, sliced
2 tablespons brown sugar
3 tablespoons soy sauce

Heat oil in skillet. When hot, brown chops on both sides. Remove from pan. Sauté onions until yellow. Return chops to pan. Add mixture of sugar and soy sauce, thinned with a little water. Cook on medium heat, covered, for 5 minutes, turning chops once. Uncover. Cook until sauce is of desired consistency.

—John Stewart

Oriental Pride Sweet and Sour Pork

The Oriental Pride Eggroll Factory in Virginia Beach processes hand-rolled lumpia eggrolls in beef, pork, and pork and shrimp, among other oriental food products. Owner Benito J. Aquino sells his frozen eggrolls, made according to a recipe of his wife's, to military installations, hospitals, schools, and commissaries. He also has a small retail store at the factory on Euclid Road. Aquino recommends the following Sweet and Sour Pork to accompany the lumpia.

Yield: 10 servings

2½ pounds pork loin, cubed
¼ cup pineapple juice
2 tablespoons soy sauce
4 egg yolks, beaten
¼ cup cornstarch
¼ pound green peppers, cut
  in 1-inch cubes
1 small can pineapple
  chunks, drained

Coating
1¼ cups cornstarch
½ teaspoon salt
½ teaspoon pepper
½ teaspoon garlic powder
1¼ teaspoons MSG
Vegetable oil as needed

Sweet and Sour Sauce
⅓ cup vinegar
½ cup sugar
½ cup ketchup
½ cup water
1½ tablespoons cornstarch
1¼ teaspoons salt

Marinate pork for 30 minutes in mixture of pineapple juice, soy sauce, egg yolks, and ¼ cup cornstarch. To make coating, mix evenly 1¼ cups cornstarch, salt, pepper, garlic powder, and MSG. Coat pork cubes in mixture and fry in oil heated to 350 degrees F. Drain and set aside. Pour off excess oil in pan and stir-fry pepper and pineapple. Mix Sweet and Sour Sauce ingredients until smooth. Add to green pepper and pineapple and stir until thickened. Add pork. Mix well and serve over rice.

—Benito J. Aquino
Oriental Pride Eggroll Factory

Wine Baked Pork Chops

Yield: 8 servings

8 pork chops, about ½ inch
  thick
Flour as needed
2 tablespoons vegetable oil
4 medium potatoes, peeled
  and quartered
½ pound fresh mushrooms,
  thinly sliced
1 large green pepper, sliced
  into strips
2 garlic cloves, minced
2 ripe tomatoes, peeled and
  quartered
¼ teaspoon oregano
¼ teaspoon sage
Salt and pepper to taste
½ cup white wine

Preheat oven to 350 degrees F. Lightly coat chops with flour. In skillet, heat oil and brown chops well on both sides. Transfer chops to large oven-proof skillet. Top with potatoes. Sauté mushrooms, peppers, and garlic in the drippings. Transfer to casserole with a slotted spoon. Top with tomatoes. Sprinkle with oregano, sage, salt, and pepper to taste. Pour wine over casserole mixture. Bake covered until chops and potatoes are tender, about 1½ hours.

—Caroline Kennett

SPOTSWOOD ARMS — VIRGINIA BEACH, VA.

Directly on the Ocean Front and Ocean Promenade   D-5163

The Spotswood Arms Hotel advertised its "Unsurpassed Old Virginia Cooked Meals" in the 1940s. Old picture postcard

Dick Cockrell on
How to Cook a Whole Hog

Dick Cockrell, director of the city's Agriculture Department, lives down in the county and has made an informal study of the variations on the theme of "pig pickin'."

A true pig pickin', he says, is when you pick the meat right off the pig with your hands, dip it in barbecue sauce, eat it, and drink bourbon. Whole hog barbecue is more refined. The meat is sliced off the pig, put on a plate, and covered with barbecue sauce; then you eat it with a fork and drink bourbon.

"You lose the atmosphere of whole hog on the coals on a chilly autumn afternoon when you do barbecue," he says. "There's more to taste than taste. You really want the crowd to see the whole hog."

He suggests making a grill with an old wire grate (old security screens from the junkyard are good) supported by six cinderblocks, three on each side. Old oil drums, cut in half, also make good grills. The top half becomes a lid and the bottom half the firebox. These can be rented, he says.

Cockrell makes his fire with charcoal, planning on one pound of charcoal per pound of meat. He says others use oak coals or gas grills (with protective shields to keep the flames away from the meat).

Whole hogs are available through local meat packing plants. A 220 to 240 pound live hog will dress out to just about enough to feed 100 people at a pig pickin'. He says you have to figure about one pound of cooked meat per person for a pickin' and about three-fourths of a pound for a barbecue. Order the hog, dressed and split in half, he says.

Prepare a good bed of coals, heated until there is no flame at any time. Keep another fire going in a barrel to replenish the cooking fire when needed. Place a steel rod through each half of the hog from shoulder to ham in order to turn the carcass. Wrap each half in chicken wire to keep the meat from falling apart.

Place both halves on the fire and cook 4 hours. Turn and cook for another 2 hours. The temperature of the grill should be about 250 degrees F. The good-old-boy way of measuring the temperature is to hold your hand where the meat is. If your hand cannot stand the heat, then the coals are too hot, Cockrell says.

Stick a butcher knife into the shoulder. If the meat is white and the shoulder joint will pull away from the meat, the hog is done. Puncture holes over the whole side and pour barbecue sauce over all, brown until golden, and serve.

Cockrell's sauce starts with a gallon of cider vinegar. He adds molasses, red pepper, Worcestershire sauce, meat sauce, salt, ketchup, and a little honey if "you want to get fancy." He says all the ingredients, excluding the vinegar, should total no more than a quart. "You just mix it to the taste of the master chef," he says.

Top Sirloin Barbecue

"Small pigs are hard to find," Cockrell says. "You have to have a buddy somewhere." So when he is serving a small crowd, he serves barbecued top sirloin. He buys a 12-to-13 pound piece, counting on about one pound per person. He cooks it 30 minutes per pound. At the fourth hour, he cuts the meat in half to get his rare piece. At the fifth hour, he cuts the well-done piece in half to get a medium piece, and at the sixth hour, the last piece is well done. For the last two hours, he adds a little sauce. Just before serving, add ketchup to the sauce and allow the fire to flame up and create a little crust.

"A good pickup truck, a good dog, a good woman, and a touch with meat, that's what makes it for a good old boy," Cockrell said.

Curried Rabbit

Every year the Fort Story Officers' Club is the site for a luncheon following the ceremony at the cross to commemorate the first landing of the settlers in Virginia Beach in 1607. The luncheon always consists of traditional food such as those eaten by the early settlers.

1 young rabbit
1 tablespoon butter
1 tablespoon vegetable oil
1 onion, chopped
1 large apple, cubed
2 tablespoons raisins
1 garlic clove, crushed
2 tablespoons coconut
¼ tablespoon chili powder
4 teaspoons curry powder
2 teaspoons thyme or
  savory
Salt and pepper to taste
1½ cups rabbit stock
1 large banana, sliced

Simmer the rabbit in water to cover until tender, about 45 minutes. Take the meat from the bones and cut into 1-inch cubes. (The bones can be returned to the stock to make it richer.) Melt the butter and oil in a heavy pot with a tight lid. Add the apple, onion, raisins, garlic, and coconut and mix well. Add the chili, curry, herbs, salt, and pepper and cook for 5 minutes, stirring often. Add the rabbit meat and stock. Cover and simmer gently for 1 hour. Add a little more stock if it becomes dry. Add the banana, stir, and cook for another 20 minutes. Serve with rice.

—Fort Story Officers' Club

The cross at Cape Henry commemorates the landing of the first settlers in 1607. Pen and ink by Janice O. Dool

Le Civet Au Lapin

La Caravelle on Laskin Road near Birdneck is responsible for introducing Virginia Beach residents to the delights of French Vietnamese cooking. This marinated rabbit is one of the unusual and delicious dishes on their menu.

Yield: 4 servings

1 fresh or frozen rabbit, cut in serving pieces
1 bottle dry red wine
Salt, pepper, and fines herbes to taste
8 slices bacon
Flour as needed
1 carrot, sliced
¼ pound mushrooms, sliced

Marinate rabbit overnight in mixture of wine, salt, pepper, and fines herbes. The next day, cook bacon and drain. Dredge carrots and mushrooms in flour and brown until golden in bacon grease. Dredge rabbit in flour and brown in grease. Place wine, rabbit, carrot, mushrooms, and crumbled bacon in casserole and simmer 2 to 3 hours until rabbit is tender. Serve with steamed new potatoes.

—La Caravelle

How to Cook a Princess Anne Turkey

Yield: 7 to 12 servings

1. Wash and clean a 14-pound Princess Anne turkey.
2. Cut out oil sack.
3. Salt inside and outside.
4. Place in roaster and add 8 cups water.
5. Bake at 350 degrees F. for 3 hours with lid on.
6. Bake at 325 degrees F. for 2 hours with lid off.
7. No basting necessary.
8. It is done when leg of turkey "jiggles" when you shake it.
9. Turkey can be stuffed, if desired. We do not stuff ours.

—Alice and Susan Flanagan

166

Princess Anne Turkeys

When people in the know in Virginia Beach talk turkey, they talk Princess Anne turkeys. The Princess Anne turkey has been a specialty of the area since at least the late 1800s.

In 1910 the Thanksgiving menu at Norfolk's Lorraine Hotel featured Virginia Beach's famed Lynnhaven oysters on the half shell and Princess Anne turkey with chestnut dressing. That same year, all the markets advertised Princess Anne turkeys in their Thanksgiving ads. Dressed, they were selling for $2.25 apiece and up.

Many of the families who farmed in the Pungo area of Princess Anne raised turkeys at the turn of the century, and the business was handed down from generation to generation. One family still in the business is the Flanagans, David and Susan, and his mother Alice, along with other relatives. By early October they can't accept another order for a Thanksgiving or Christmas turkey. Some of their customers go back for ten to fifteen years. They place their orders for next year's turkey when they pick up this year's turkey.

Princess Anne turkeys might be called the original self-basting turkey. They are so naturally fat they never need basting. The Flanagans say the turkeys are so good because they are raised the old-fashioned way—outside on the ground. In the morning the turkeys are fed turkey feed just like ordinary turkeys are fed, but in the afternoon the original Princess Anne turkey gets a meal of whole corn—"bucketsful of beautiful yellow corn," Alice Flanagan says.

With care like that, it's no wonder that Princess Anne turkeys are good enough to provoke Virginia Beach residents in the know to talk turkey.

Princess Anne Turkey Dressing

Yield: enough for 12- to 14-pound turkey

1 cup celery, chopped
1 cup onion, chopped
1 loaf of bread, toasted and
   cut in cubes
Turkey giblets, cooked and
   cut up
1 cup sausage meat, cooked
   and drained
2 hard-cooked eggs,
   chopped
Salt and pepper to taste
Turkey or chicken stock as
   needed

Preheat oven to 350 degrees F. Sauté celery and onion until onions are translucent. Mix all ingredients together, moistening them with turkey stock. Make into patties about 1 tablespoon each and bake on a cookie sheet for about 30 minutes or until brown on top.

—Alice Flanagan

Veal with Mustard

Yield: 2 servings

Veal cutlets for two,
   pounded to ¼-inch
   thickness
Butter
¼ cup minced shallots
   (scallions will do)
½ cup dry white wine
½ cup chicken stock or
   broth
¼ cup heavy cream
4 tablespoons good
   mustard
2 tablespoons chopped
   fresh parsley

Season veal cutlets with salt and pepper; sauté briefly in butter over medium high heat, adding butter when necessary. Remove cutlets and keep warm.

Add shallots to skillet and sauté until soft. Add wine and chicken stock in equal proportions. Increase heat until sauce begins to thicken. Stir in cream and reduce to desired consistency for sauce. Add mustard to taste. Add chopped parsley, blend to smooth consistency, and serve over veal.

—Joe Lyle

Grains

Lighting the bonfires at Cape Henry to guide the ships through the Virginia capes before the lighthouse was built. Drawing by Polly Blackford. Courtesy of the Virginia Beach Maritime Historical Museum

Admirable Success with Grains

"Indian corn, wheat, oats, and rye grow well. Wheat is not grown to any extent, the general impression being the climate is too damp; but some of our best farmers have succeeded admirably with wheat. Grasses grow well especially red clover."

—America. *Homes for Englishmen in the State of Virginia*
a real estate brochure on Princess Anne County, 1872

Sally Lunn Bread

This recipe is around 100 years old.

Yield: 1 tube loaf

1 yeast cake
¼ cup milk, warmed
⅔ cup sugar
3 eggs
⅜ cup melted butter or
  margarine
⅜ cup vegetable shortening,
  melted
1¼ cup milk
2 teaspoons salt
4 cups flour

Dissolve 1 yeast cake with ¼ cup warm milk and 1 heaping tablespoon sugar taken from amount above (set aside). Beat eggs with remaining sugar. Mix melted butter and shortening and add to the beaten eggs. Add the cup of warm milk to the mixture. Sift 4 cups flour with 2 level teaspoons salt and set aside. Mix yeast mixture with other liquids. Be sure liquids are only tepid before you put the yeast mixture into it. Stir liquid mixture into flour and salt. Mix well and place in a warm place—not too warm. Let rise 2 hours. Stir vigorously and put into well-greased tube pan. Put aside for 2 more hours in the tube pan and let rise. Then put in 250 degree F. oven for 10 minutes. Increase heat 25 degrees every 5 minutes until 375 degrees F. is reached. Bake 45 minutes. Turn off electricity and let stay in oven for 10 minutes. When crust begins to form, brush with melted butter. Let stand outside oven 5 minutes. Turn out quickly to avoid broken crust.

—Johnnie S. Miller

Potato Rolls

Yield: about 6 dozen rolls

1 package dry yeast
½ cup sugar
3 cups warm water
1 teaspoon salt
4 tablespoons vegetable
  shortening
2 cups mashed potatoes
6 cups flour, sifted

Add yeast and sugar to the water. Mix salt, shortening, and potatoes with the flour and add to the liquid. Knead. Let dough rise until double in bulk then form into rolls and let rise until very light. Preheat oven to 350 degrees F. Bake about 20 minutes, or until browned.

—Effie Munden

Eastern Shore Chapel
Whole Wheat Bread

This recipe for bread is one of those used in the communion service at Eastern Shore Chapel on Laskin Road. Despite four major changes in its structure, Eastern Shore Chapel has managed to serve Episcopalians in Virginia Beach continuously for more than 300 years, longer than any other church in the area. The church was established in the 1600s when it was built as a chapel in the Lynnhaven Parish. The first major structure was built in the 1750s and remained in its location south of Oceana until the Naval Air Station expanded in the 1950s. The present church was built in the same design, using some of the original bricks and stained glass windows.

Yield: 2 loaves

5½ to 6 cups unsifted white flour, divided
2 cups unsifted whole wheat flour
3 tablespoons sugar
4 teaspoons salt
2 packages dry yeast
2 cups milk
¾ cup water
4 tablespoons butter or margarine
Vegetable oil as needed

Combine flours. In a large bowl thoroughly mix 2½ cups flour mixture, sugar, salt, and undissolved yeast. Combine milk, water, and butter in a saucepan. Heat over low heat until liquids are very warm (120 to 130 degrees F.). Butter does not need to melt. Gradually add to dry ingredients and beat with electric mixer 2 minutes at medium speed, scraping bowl occasionally. Add 1 cup flour mixture. Beat at high speed 2 minutes, scraping bowl occasionally. Stir in enough additional flour mixture to make a stiff dough. Turn out onto lightly floured board and knead until smooth and elastic, about 8 to 10 minutes. Cover with plastic wrap and then a towel. Let rest 20 minutes.

Divide dough in half. Roll each half into a 14-by-9-inch rectangle. Shape into loaves by rolling tightly from narrow end. Seal ends and fold under. Place in two greased 9-by-5-by-3-inch loaf pans. Brush loaves with oil and cover with plastic wrap. Refrigerate 2 to 24 hours.

When ready to bake, remove from refrigerator. Uncover dough carefully. Preheat oven to 400 degrees F. Let stand at room temperature 10 minutes. Puncture any gas bubbles which may have formed with a greased toothpick or metal skewer. Bake about 40 minutes, or until done. Remove from pans and cool on wire racks.

—Eastern Shore Chapel Episcopal Church

Cardamom Christmas Muffins

Yield: 1 dozen

1¾ cups flour
½ cup sugar
2 teaspoons baking powder
½ teaspoon cardamom
2 eggs, beaten
4 tablespoons melted butter
¾ cup milk
½ cup mixed candied fruit
½ cup raisins or currants

Preheat oven to 400 degrees F. Mix dry ingredients in bowl. Add butter and milk to eggs and mix. Add liquid ingredients to flour mixture quickly and stir just a few seconds. Fold in fruits and raisins or currants. Fill well-greased muffin tins three-quarters full and bake for 20 to 25 minutes.
—Mary Reid Barrow

Emma Cora's Split Biscuits

This recipe belonged to Katie Miller's grandmother. Mrs. Miller still makes the rolls today, but she doesn't always adhere as carefully to the time limits imposed by her grandmother!

Yield: about 4 dozen

½ cup sugar
1 cup hot, lightly packed
    mashed white potatoes
1 yeast cake
½ cup (1 stick) butter
½ cup lard
½ cup sweet milk, warmed
6 cups flour
2 teaspoons salt

Place sugar in bowl with mashed potatoes. Dissolve yeast and melt butter and lard in warm milk. Add to mashed potato mixture. Add 4 cups flour and salt and mix. Let rise from 9 a.m. to noon. Work over using 2 cups flour. Set to rise until 4 p.m. Preheat oven to 350 degrees F. Work over and roll out ⅜-inch thick. Cut with biscuit cutter. Layer two biscuits together on a greased cookie sheet, brushing the bottom biscuit with butter. Bake 12 to 15 minutes or until brown.
—Katie Miller

Eastern Shore Chapel Egg Bread

This is one of the breads used at the church's communion service.

Yield: 3 loaves

6¾ to 7 cups flour, divided
2 packages dry yeast
2 cups milk
4 tablespoons butter or
　margarine
¼ cup granulated sugar
1 tablespoon salt
3 eggs

In a large mixer bowl, combine 3 cups flour and yeast. In saucepan, heat the milk, butter or margarine, granulated sugar, and salt just until warm (115 to 120 degrees F.), stirring constantly until butter almost melts. Add dry ingredients in mixer bowl; add eggs. With electric mixer, beat at low speed for ½ minute, scraping sides of bowl constantly. Beat 3 minutes at high speed. By hand, stir in just enough of the remaining flour to make a moderately stiff dough. Turn out onto floured surface and knead until smooth and elastic, 5 to 8 minutes. Place in greased bowl, turning once to grease surface. Cover; let rise until double, about 1 hour. Divide dough in three parts. Let rest 10 minutes, covered. Shape dough into loaves and place in three greased 9-by-5-inch loaf pans. Cover and let loaves rise until double, about 1 hour. Preheat oven to 375 degrees F. Gently brush tops with mixture of 1 beaten egg and 1 tablespoon water. Bake loaves for 20 to 25 minutes. Turn out onto racks and cool.

—Eastern Shore Chapel Episcopal Church

Mama's Rolls

Yield: 6 dozen rolls

3 tablespoons vegetable
　shortening
1 tablespoon salt
3 tablespoons sugar
1 cup hot water
1 yeast cake
½ cup warm water
½ cup canned milk
6 cups flour

Put shortening, salt, and sugar in large bowl. Pour in 1 cup hot water, mix all, and let cool. Dissolve yeast in ½ cup water; add ½ cup milk to yeast mixture. Add yeast mixture to large bowl contents. Add flour and knead. Place in greased bowl and cover. Let rise until double. Make rolls. Place in greased pans and let rise until light. Bake at 400 degrees F. for about 20 minutes.

—Phyllis Dowdy
Country Roads Cookbook, 1981

Mrs. Smith's Batterbread

Yield: 6 to 8 servings

1 cup cornmeal, yellow or
　white
3 cups milk
2 teaspoons vegetable
　shortening
3 eggs, beaten
1½ teaspoons salt
3 teaspoons baking powder

Preheat oven to 400 degrees F. Stir together cornmeal and 2 cups milk in a pan until smooth. Add shortening. Bring to a boil, stirring constantly. Combine beaten eggs, salt, and remaining milk. Add to cornmeal mixture and stir well. Stir in baking powder. Pour into 1½- or 2-quart greased casserole. Bake for 30 to 45 minutes.

—Isabel Dunn

Sallie's Beaten Biscuits

Yield: about 4 dozen

1 quart flour
1¾ teaspoons salt
2 ounces (2 tablespoons)
　lard or vegetable
　shortening
1 tumbler of ½ milk and
　½ water

Make a stiff dough and beat for ½ hour until it blisters. Roll out and cut with a small cutter. Prick with silver fork. Bake at 350 degrees F. about 25 minutes or until faintly colored, not browned.

—Ruth Barrow

Buckwheat Cakes

Yield: about 2 dozen

3 cups lukewarm water
1 package yeast
3 cups buckwheat flour
1 tablespoon molasses
1 teaspoon salt
1 teaspoon baking powder

Dissolve yeast in water. Add flour and mix well. Let rise for several hours, overnight if possible. Add the molasses, salt, and baking powder before cooking. Cook on a hot well-greased griddle. If batter is too thick, thin with water.

—Virginia Dyer

176

Mercer's Boathouse Cornbread

This is a luncheon favorite of the Princess Anne Courthouse crowd at Mercer's Boathouse on the North Landing River.

Yield: 6 servings

1 hamburger roll
½ cup hot water
½ cup (1 stick) butter or
  margarine
1 cup self-rising cornmeal
1 teaspoon salt
2 tablespoons sugar
1 cup milk
2 eggs

Preheat oven to 400 degrees F. Scald hamburger roll with ½ cup hot water and set aside to cool. Put butter in glass Pyrex 8-by-8-inch dish or pan, melt, and set aside. Mix remaining ingredients with cooled hamburger roll. Pour into butter. Cook until golden brown.

—Vivian Mercer

Page Davis's Cornbread

Yield: 1 dozen muffins

1 cup cornmeal
1 cup wheat flour
½ teaspoon salt
½ teaspoon baking soda
1 egg
1½ cups buttermilk

Preheat cast iron skillet or muffin pan to 425 degrees F. Mix cornmeal, flour, salt, and baking soda. Add egg and buttermilk. Put dot of butter in pan, or a quick spray of "Pam." Bake for 25 minutes.

Hint: Use an ice cream scoop to fill muffin pan quickly and evenly.

—Page Davis

Norah Morris's Corn Griddle Cakes

Yield: 4 to 6 servings

1 cup white cornmeal
2 cups boiling water
1 teaspoon salt
2 teaspoons sugar
1 egg
About ½ cup milk
1 tablespoon flour
1 teaspoon baking powder

Scald cornmeal with boiling water. Add salt and sugar and beat in egg. Add as much milk as necessary for a thin batter. Sift flour with baking powder and add just before cooking on a hot griddle.

—Alice McCaw

Cornmeal Cakes

Yield: 4 servings

1 egg
1 cup water-ground
   cornmeal
1 to 2 cups milk
½ to 1 cup boiling water
1 teaspoon salt
½ to 1 stick butter or
   margarine, melted
1 teaspoon baking powder

Beat the egg. Add the cornmeal and mix until all lumps are out. Add enough milk to just moisten. Cover with boiling water and mix well. Add enough milk to make thin batter. Add salt, melted butter, and baking powder. Cook on a very hot, well-greased griddle.

—Virginia Dyer

Ethel's Pancakes

This pancake recipe was a favorite of Margaret Eady's when she was growing up at Pembroke Manor. For many years Ethel Nichols was the family cook. Pembroke Manor was once an elegant plantation owned by British Tory John Saunders who was forced to flee to Canada during the Revolutionary War. The handsome home passed through a succession of owners until the Princess Anne County Historical Society purchased it in 1963 and began the slow, expensive process of restoration.

Yield: 2 servings

2 slices bread
1 cup milk
1 tablespoon baking powder
¼ cup flour
¼ cup cornmeal
1 egg, beaten
¼ teaspoon salt
½ teaspoon sugar
3 tablespoons melted butter

Break bread in several pieces into milk. Soak overnight in refrigerator. The next morning, add remaining ingredients and stir well. Drop batter on hot griddle and cook as you would pancakes.

—Margaret Eady

Oatmeal Pancakes

Yield: 4 to 5 servings

¾ cup regular or quick-cooking oatmeal, uncooked
1½ cups milk, skim or whole
2 eggs, beaten
¼ cup melted vegetable shortening, cooled
1¼ cups flour
2 tablespoons sugar
1 tablespoon baking powder
1 teaspoon salt (optional)
¼ cup wheat germ (optional)

Combine oatmeal and milk; let set 5 minutes. Add eggs and shortening to oat mixture, mixing well. Combine dry ingredients and add to oat mixture. Stir until just blended. Pour ⅛ to ¼ cup on hot griddle for each pancake. When surfaces are bubbly and edges slightly dry, turn and cook other side.

—Susan Kolodny

Old Princess Anne Hotel Pancakes

Early on the morning of June 10, 1907 the original Princess Anne Hotel was leveled within fifteen minutes by a fire originating in the kitchen. The elegant structure with its high-ceilinged, wood-paneled dining room was a favorite resort hotel for the likes of many famous people from presidents to theatrical celebrities. The hotel began as the Virginia Beach Hotel which opened its doors in 1883 when the first rail line inaugurated service to the Beach. In 1922 the tradition of the Princess Anne Hotel was carried on when a new hotel was built on 25th Street and was purchased a year later by the Sterling family. In 1963 the second Princess Anne Hotel was torn down to make way for the Princess Anne Inn which is still operated today by the Sterlings. Perhaps these rich pancakes were the cause of the 1907 fire!

Yield: 2 dozen pancakes

5 eggs
1 cup (2 sticks) melted butter
2 cups milk, less if thick pancakes are desired
½ cup sugar
2 cups flour
4 teaspoons baking powder
Dash salt

Beat eggs. Add melted butter and milk. Mix sugar, flour, baking powder, and salt; add to egg mixture. Stir until lumps are gone. Right before cooking, blend in blender until light and airy.

—Alice Sterling Mullen

The Virginia Beach Hotel, built in 1883, was the first hotel at the beach. Courtesy of the Virginia State Library

Dainty Tea Cookies

Betty Michelson says this is her mother's favorite cookie recipe—a great little extra at Christmas.

Yield: about 3 dozen

¾ cup butter, at room
   temperature
¼ cup vegetable shortening
⅔ cup sugar
1 egg
2½ cups flour
½ teaspoon salt
1 teaspoon almond extract

Preheat oven to 350 degrees F. Cream butter, shortening, and sugar together. Add egg and mix thoroughly. Add dry ingredients which have been sifted together. Add vanilla. Put through cookie press onto greased cookie sheet. Bake for about 6 minutes.

—Betty Michelson

Chocolate Bittersweets

Yield: about 2 dozen

Cookie
½ cup (1 stick) butter
½ cup confectioner's sugar
¼ teaspoon salt
1 teaspoon vanilla extract
1 to 1¼ cups flour

Filling
3 ounces cream cheese
1 cup sifted confectioner's
   sugar
2 tablespoons flour
1 teaspoon vanilla extract
½ cup finely chopped
   walnuts
½ cup flake coconut

Frosting
½ cup semi-sweet chocolate
   drops
2 tablespoons butter
2 tablespoons water
½ cup sifted confectioner's
   sugar

Preheat oven to 350 degrees F. Cream butter and sugar until light and fluffy. Add salt and vanilla. Cream well. Gradually add flour. Shape into balls. Place on ungreased cookie sheet. Press a hole in the center of each cookie. Bake 12 to 15 minutes until delicately brown. Fill while warm with filling.

To make filling: Blend cream cheese with sugar, flour, and vanilla. Cream well. Stir in walnuts and coconut. When cool ice with frosting.

To make frosting: Melt chocolate drops with butter and water over low heat, stirring occasionally. Add sugar and beat until smooth.

—Betty Michelson

Courthouse Brownies

Every year the circuit court clerk's office at Princess Anne Courthouse hosts a Christmas luncheon for the courthouse crowd. The courthouse is the sixth courthouse Princess Anne County has had, yet it has served longer than any of the other five. The first three were in the Lynnhaven area, the fourth in Newtown, and the fifth was built in Kempsville following the Revolutionary War. In 1820, however, the Virginia General Assembly passed legislation entitled "An act for changing the place of holding courts for the county of Princess Anne." And in 1820 a group of commissioners entered into a contract with a builder to construct the courthouse complex in a "strong, neat, faithful, and workmanlike manner." In 1920 the courthouse was restored and still is in use today with some modern additions. It sets the tone both architecturally and figuratively for the rest of the city's governmental complex.

The Christmas luncheon in the circuit court setting with Mary Cooper's brownies and other covered dishes from some of the best Princess Anne County cooks combines the best of two worlds.

Yield: 1 dozen

½ cup (1 stick) butter, at room temperature
1 cup sugar
2 eggs
1 teaspoon vanilla extract
½ cup flour
2 squares unsweetened chocolate, melted
½ cup chopped nuts

Fudge Frosting
1 cup sifted confectioner's sugar
1 tablespoon cocoa
2 tablespoons light cream
1 tablespoon butter

Preheat oven to 325 degrees F. Thoroughly cream butter and sugar. Add eggs and vanilla and beat thoroughly. Add flour. Blend in chocolate and nuts. Pour batter into a greased 8-by-8-inch baking pan. Clean out bowl with a rubber scraper. Bake 35 minutes. When the brownies are done, lightly press around the edges of the pan with the bottom of a glass to make the top level. Cool. Spread with Fudge Frosting, made by combining sugar, cocoa, cream, and butter in saucepan and cooking until the mixture boils around the side of the pan. Remove from the heat and beat until the frosting is of spreading consistency.

—Mary Cooper

Kay Moore's Christmas Sugar Cookies

Yield: about 2 dozen

1 cup (2 sticks) butter, at
   room temperature
1 cup sugar
2 eggs
1 tablespoon milk
½ teaspoon vanilla extract
½ teaspoon salt
1 teaspoon baking powder
1½ cups flour
Colored sugar or nuts

Cream butter and sugar. Add eggs, milk, vanilla, and salt. Sift together the baking powder and flour and add to butter mixture. Roll in ball and chill in refrigerator. Preheat oven to 375 degrees F. With floured rolling pin and a large amount of flour on board, roll out a small amount of dough. Cut with cookie cutter or wine glass. Sprinkle colored sugar or press piece of walnut or half a pecan in center to decorate. Bake about 8 minutes on greased cookie sheet. Keep dough in refrigerator while rolling out the part you are using.

—Hannah Moore

Princess Anne Courthouse, Virginia Beach, Virginia

Princess Anne Courthouse was built in 1823 and sets the tone both figuratively and architecturally for the municipal complex. Courtesy of the Virginia Beach Bank of Commerce

Eastern Shore Chapel
Gingerbread Men

These gingerbread men are decorated by Eastern Shore Chapel's Sunday School children for sale at the bazaar.

Yield: 15 to 20 large gingerbread men

1 cup (2 sticks) butter or
   margarine, at room
   temperature
⅔ cup packed brown sugar
½ cup light molasses
1 egg
3½ cups flour
1 teaspoon salt
1 teaspoon baking powder
1 teaspoon ground ginger
1 teaspoon ground allspice
1 teaspoon ground
   cinnamon
1 teaspoon ground cloves

Up to one week ahead: In large bowl with mixer at low speed, beat butter or margarine, brown sugar, and molasses until light and fluffy. Add egg and remaining ingredients. Beat at low speed until well mixed, constantly scraping bowl with rubber spatula. Shape dough into a ball; wrap dough with plastic wrap or waxed paper and refrigerate 3 to 4 hours until firm. Preheat oven to 350 degrees F. Lightly grease two large cookie sheets. Cut dough in half. On lightly floured surface with lightly floured rolling pin, roll one half of dough ¼ inch thick (keep remaining dough refrigerated). With large gingerbread man cookie cutter, cut as many cookies as possible; reserve trimmings. With pancake turner, carefully place cookies on cookie sheets. Bake 12 minutes or until edges of cookies are lightly browned. Remove cookies to wire racks to cool. Repeat with remaining dough and reroll trimmings. Prepare frosting "paint."

To decorate gingerbread men place cookies on waxed-paper-lined cookie sheets. With small and medium artist's brushes and decorating tubes, decorate gingerbread people as desired. Set aside to allow frosting to dry completely, about 2 hours.

Frosting "Paint"
2½ cups confectioner's
   sugar
¼ teaspoon cream of tartar
2 egg whites
Food coloring

In large bowl with mixer at low speed, beat sugar, cream of tartar, and egg whites until just mixed. Increase speed to high and beat until mixture is stiff and knife drawn through mixture leaves a clean-cut path. Divide frosting into small bowls. Tint each bowl of frosting with food coloring as desired, and if necessary, add a little water so icing will spread easily. Keep all bowls covered with plastic wrap to prevent frosting from drying out.

—Holy Chow Bazaar Bake Shop,
Eastern Shore Chapel

Family Tea Cookies

These cookies are a favorite at Christmas time for Mr. and Mrs. Sidney Kellam and their family. Mr. Kellam, a powerful political figure for many years, provided the leadership for the merger of Princess Anne County and Virginia Beach in 1963.

Yield: 4 to 5 dozen

1 cup (2 sticks) butter, at
   room temperature
½ cup confectioner's sugar
1 teaspoon vanilla extract
2 cups flour
1 cup chopped pecans

Preheat oven to 325 degrees F. Cream butter and sugar. Add vanilla, flour, and nuts. Roll into balls. Chill. Bake on ungreased cookie sheet for 20 minutes or until slightly browned. While still warm, roll in confectioner's sugar.

—Odie Kellam

Koulourakia
(Cinnamon Cookie Twists)

This is a favorite at the annual Greek festival at Saint Nicholas Greek Orthodox Church on First Colonial Road.

Yield: 6 dozen

1 pound (4 sticks) butter, at
    room temperature
2½ cups sugar
6 eggs
5 teaspoons baking powder
1 teaspoon baking soda
3 teaspoons cinnamon
2½ to 3 pounds flour,
    divided
¼ cup olive oil
1 egg yolk

Preheat oven to 350 degrees F. Cream butter for 15 minutes. Add sugar, creaming well. Add eggs, one at a time, beating constantly. Combine baking powder, soda, cinnamon, and about 4 cups flour and add to mixture. When well blended, add oil and more flour until mix will roll easily in palm of hand without sticking. Make little cookies in shapes such as braids and wreaths. Brush tops with beaten egg yolk thinned with a little milk. Bake on greased cookie sheet for 30 minutes or until nicely browned.

—Helen J. Christie

Emily's Molasses Cookies

Yield: 60 cookies

1 cup sugar
1 teaspoon ginger
2 teaspoons cinnamon
Pinch salt
1 cup molasses
1 egg, beaten
1 tablespoon vanilla extract
1 cup vegetable shortening,
    melted (keep warm)
⅔ cup water
1 teaspoon cream of tartar
3 teaspoons baking soda
5 cups flour, sifted

Preheat oven to 375 degrees F. Mix together sugar, ginger, cinnamon, and salt. Add molasses, egg, and vanilla. Add shortening. Mix cream of tartar and baking soda in water and add. Add flour 1 cup at a time. Mix quite stiff to roll. Cut with cookie cutter. Cook for 7½ minutes.

Helpful Hint: Let mixture stand for ½ to 1 hour. Rolls out better, using less flour.

—Emily Davis

Myrtle's Divine Chocolate Cake

Yield: 1 10½-by-15½-inch sheet cake

2 cups flour
2 cups sugar
1 teaspoon baking soda
¼ teaspoon salt
½ cup (1 stick) butter
½ cup vegetable oil
1 cup water or coffee
¼ cup cocoa
2 eggs
1 teaspoon vanilla extract
½ cup buttermilk or
    sour cream

Icing
1 cup sugar
½ cup (1 stick) butter
⅓ cup evaporated milk
½ cup chocolate chips

Butter and flour a 10½-by-15½-inch jelly roll pan. Preheat oven to 350 degrees F. Place flour, sugar, baking soda, and salt in large bowl. Heat butter, oil, water or coffee, and cocoa in saucepan and bring just to a boil. Pour over dry ingredients and beat until smooth. Add eggs, vanilla, and buttermilk or sour cream. Beat until just smooth. Do not over-beat. Bake in prepared pan for about 20 minutes. If your oven is not perfectly even, carefully turn the pan around after 8 or 9 minutes of baking. While the cake is baking, prepare the icing. In a pan cook sugar with butter and milk. When it comes to a boil, lower heat and add chocolate chips. Cook gently for 3 minutes, stirring. Pour over entire sheet cake. Allow to cool before slicing.

—Margene Sullivan

Hot Milk Cake

Yield: 1 tube cake

1 cup hot milk
½ cup (1 stick) butter
4 eggs
2 cups sugar
2 cups flour
1 teaspoon baking powder
½ teaspoon salt
1 teaspoon vanilla extract

Preheat oven to 350 degrees F. Melt butter with milk, bringing almost to a boil, then cool. Beat eggs and sugar together; add flour, salt, and baking powder. Then fold in butter, milk, and vanilla. Bake in a tube pan for 1 hour.

—Norma Hunter

Brian's Easy Chocolate Cake

Brian was the baker on the pilot boat *Virginia*. He was formerly the pastry chef at the Omni International Hotel.

Yield: 1 cake

2 cups flour
2 cups sugar
¾ cup Hershey's cocoa
1 cup milk
2 teaspoons baking soda
1 teaspoon baking powder
2 eggs
1 cup boiling water
½ cup (1 stick) butter

Preheat oven to 350 degrees F. Combine all ingredients except boiling water and butter. Add water and butter exactly and carefully into mixture. Bake for 30 minutes.

—Bob Callis
Loaves and Fishes, III
Galilee Church

Old-Fashioned Jelly Roll

Yield: 1 jelly roll

¾ cup sifted cake flour
¾ teaspoon baking powder
¼ teaspoon salt
4 eggs
¾ cup sifted sugar
1 teaspoon vanilla extract
1 cup jelly (favorite flavor)

Preheat oven to 400 degrees F. Combine baking powder, salt, and eggs in bowl. Place over small bowl of hot water and beat with rotary egg beater, adding sugar gradually until mixture becomes thick and light colored. Remove bowl from hot water. Fold in flour and vanilla. Turn into 15-by-10-inch pan which has been greased, lined with heavy brown paper to within ½ inch of edge, and greased again. Bake about 13 minutes. Remove from oven and quickly cut off any crisp edges. Turn out on cloth covered with confectioner's sugar. Remove paper. Spread with jelly and roll with aid of cloth. Wrap in cloth and cool on rack.

—Betty Michelson

Mary Cooper's Plain Cake

Yield: 1 10-inch tube cake

1 cup (2 sticks) butter, at
    room temperature
3 cups sugar
3 cups flour
1 cup milk
1 teaspoon lemon extract
5 eggs
½ teaspoon baking powder
1 teaspoon vanilla extract
⅛ teaspoon salt

Cream butter and sugar well. Add 1 egg at a time, beating well after each addition. Add flour, baking powder, milk, and flavoring slowly, a small amount at a time, and beat well. Grease tube pan with butter. This cake may be baked two ways:

1. Put in cold oven set at 300 degrees F. Cook 1 hour and 40 minutes.
2. Cook for 1 hour and 15 minutes in a preheated 350 degree F. oven. Turn off oven after 1 hour and leave in the oven the remaining 15 minutes.

Frost with seven-minute frosting.

—Mary Cooper

Seven-Minute Frosting

2 egg whites
4 tablespoons white syrup
2 cups sugar
4 tablespoons water
1 teaspoon vanilla extract

Cook first four ingredients in double boiler for 7 minutes. Beat with an electric mixer at high speed while cooking until mixture stands in high peaks. Add vanilla after removing from heat. Spread on cake.

—Mary Cooper

Fran's Pound Cake

This 100-year-old recipe is included in a *Resume of Recipes from Members of the Council of Garden Clubs of Virginia Beach, Inc.* The council has been in existence since 1950 and has any number of city beautification projects to their credit, many of them at historical sites. Club projects include the Colonial Garden at the Municipal Center, the Herb Garden at the Francis Land House, the Norwegian Lady Plaza, and the landscaping on Atlantic Avenue.

Yield: 1 tube cake

1 pound creamery butter
3⅓ cups sugar
10 large eggs
4 cups flour
1 teaspoon vanilla extract

Have all ingredients at room temperature. In large bowl, cream butter and sugar well with mixer. Add eggs one at a time, mixing well. Add vanilla and flour and mix well. Pour into greased tube pan and start in COLD oven set for 350 degrees F. Bake for 30 minutes. Reduce heat to 325 degrees F. and cook about 1 hour and 15 to 20 minutes. Do not undercook. This cake freezes very well and some think it is even better after being frozen.
—Fran Vowell, Linkhorn Park Garden Club
Resume of Recipes from Members of the Council of Garden Clubs of Virginia Beach, Inc., 1980

Christmas: A Time to Make Merry

When Adam Thoroughgood arrived here in the 1630s, he was settling in a foreign land, full of unknowns. Fears of Indians, illnesses, the cold, and hunger must have cast a shadow on every day of the year, including Christmas.

The Christmas tree didn't come to Virginia Beach until the 1800s and gift giving, other than alms, was not a tradition either. Therefore Christmas dinner, if the harvest had been good, would have been the highlight of the Thoroughgoods' secular celebration.

The menu would have included bounty peculiar to American shores such as oysters and wildfowl. An English tradition such as plum pudding would have been rare because the fruits would have been so hard to come by. Adam may have mixed a wassail bowl, however. Made of hot ale, spices, and apples, wassail comes from the old English phrase, "We thou well."

Captain John Smith in his diary confirms the Christmas repasts enjoyed by early Virginians. One Christmas he set out on a raid against the Indians and wrote:

"The extreme wind, rayne, frost and snow caused us to keep Christmas among the savages, where we were never more merry, nor fed on more plenty of good Oysters, Fish, Flesh, Wilde fowl and good bread, nor never had better fires in England."

Christmas in the 1600s may not have been a magical time, but it was an occasion to eat, drink, and be merry.

Lynnhaven House Bread Pudding

Lynnhaven House, owned by the Association for the Preservation of Virginia Antiquities, is one of the most important early eighteenth-century structures to still survive in Virginia. Built around 1725, the home was constructed during the last years of property owner Francis Thelaball, a typical merchant/farmer in the area. Former Lynnhaven House Administrator Paula Opheim developed this recipe for bread pudding to be used in hearthside cooking demonstrations in the huge original fireplace at Lynnhaven House.

Yield: 12 servings

4 cups cubed stale bread
  (brown and white bread
  mixed)
½ to 1 cup honey to taste
5 eggs, beaten
1 quart milk
1 tablespoon vanilla extract
Pinch salt
¼ to ½ cup brown sugar
¾ cup raisins or other fruit
  such as leftover fried
  apples
Nutmeg as needed

In a large bowl mix bread cubes with honey and allow to sit until bread absorbs honey. Add milk, vanilla, salt, and brown sugar to eggs. Add egg mixture to the breadcrumbs and honey. Add fruit.

For open-hearth cooking: Grease a dutch oven and the inside of its lid. Pour in the pudding. Sprinkle grated nutmeg over the top. Place the lid on and bake on a bed of coals with coals on top of the lid also for 1½ hours or until the lid begins to rise and you can smell the pudding.

For modern oven: Preheat oven to 350 degrees F. Grease a large casserole. Pour in pudding. Sprinkle nutmeg on top. Set dish in a pan of water and bake for 1 hour or more until pudding tests done in the center.

—Paula Opheim

The Wishart House, now known as the Lynnhaven House, was built in the 1720s and is owned by the Virginia Association for the Preservation of Virginia Antiquities and is open to the public. Pen and ink by Janice O. Dool

Old Homestead Pudding

Yield: 12 "muffins"

4 tablespoons butter, at
    room temperature
½ cup sugar
1 egg, beaten
1 cup flour
2 teaspoons baking powder
Pinch salt
½ cup milk
1 teaspoon vanilla extract

Sauce
2 eggs
1 cup sugar
1 cup heavy cream,
    whipped
Vanilla extract, rum, sherry,
    or other flavoring to taste

Preheat oven to 375 degrees F. Cream butter and sugar. Add egg and beat. Sift flour, baking powder, and salt together and add to butter mixture alternating with milk and vanilla. Fill greased muffin tins three-quarters full and bake 15 minutes. Serve very hot with this very cold sauce.

To make sauce, beat eggs well. Add sugar and beat until fairly thick. Add cream and whatever flavoring you prefer. The sauce can be made ahead of time, but the pudding (other than creaming the butter and sugar) must be mixed and put in the oven right away.

—Janet Werndli

193

Sallie's Plum Pudding

Yield: 1 8-cup mold

1 cup breadcrumbs
1 cup finely chopped suet
¾ cup brown sugar, firmly
    packed
2 cups raisins
½ cup chopped nuts
½ cup citron
½ cup flour
½ teaspoon *each* nutmeg,
    cinnamon, allspice, mace,
    and salt
2 teaspoons baking powder
2 well-beaten eggs
1 cup milk

Mix breadcrumbs, suet, brown sugar, raisins, nuts, and citron in bowl. Sift flour, spices, and baking powder into fruit mixture and stir. Add beaten eggs and milk. Pour into well-greased mold and tie a piece of waxed paper around the top. Steam for 3 hours on top of the stove.

—Ruth Barrow

MUNDEN'S GROCERY, PUNGO

MARY LYNN PERNEY
12-21-82

Munden's Grocery in Pungo is an old-fashioned general store. Drawing by Mary Lynn Perney

Wild Things

A scenic bridge overlooks a cypress pond at Seashore State Park.
Courtesy of the Virginia State Parks Division

Where the Wild Things Thrive

Virginia Beach is anchored at its northern end by Seashore State Park where, though open to the public for certain forms of recreation, the animal and plant life comes first.

The area always was prized for its abundance of fish and game and in the 1700s colonists began applying for the patents on the land. Fishermen who camped there protested to the government. They asked "that the land remain a common for the benefit of the inhabitants of the colony." From that day forward, the area has been owned by the state except for a brief period in the late 1800s.

Even before the settlers arrived, the Indians took advantage of the area's unique assets. They used it as their hunting and fishing grounds. They gathered oysters from its surrounding waters and blueberries from its bushes. They made canoes from its cypress trees and diapers for their babies from its Spanish moss.

Early settlers also enjoyed the blueberries and oysters. In addition, they gathered blackberrries, persimmons, and wild grapes. And they learned from the Indians how to use the little partridge berry as a home remedy. They distilled the oil from the leaves, added honey, and made a cure for coughs and sore throats. They also steamed the leaves in hot water to make a delicious tea.

Early sailors and pirates alike used the fresh water from the ponds to replenish their water supplies. Tannic acid from oak bark acted as a preservative for the pond water and made it especially suited for long ocean voyages.

In 1936 a group of conservative-minded citizens were successful in persuading the state to establish the area as a state park. Conservationists

197

still keep a wary eye on the area to ensure the preservation of its 2,710 acres of flora and fauna in the midst of one of the fastest growing cities in the United States.

In 1607 after landing at Cape Henry, one of the settlers, George Percy, recorded the events in his diary. Seashore State Park was in his mind's eye when he wrote: "Heaven and earth never agreed better to frame a place for man's habitation than Virginia."

Bayberry Tea

Yield: 4 to 6 servings per quart

15 bayberry leaves per quart
of water
2 tablespoons honey

Steep leaves in boiling water for 10 minutes. Add honey and chill.

—Vicki Shufer

Blackberry Pudding of Colonial Days

½ pound butter
½ pound flour
1 pound brown sugar
4 eggs (beat very light)

Cream the butter and sugar together until light. Add the well-beaten eggs and twice-sifted flour alternately. Put into a baking dish and add one heaping quart of fresh blackberries. Bake as you would a pound cake. Serve hot or cold with wine sauce.

Wine Sauce: 1 pound of sugar and ½ pound of butter creamed together, and made warm but not hot. Add 1 pint of sherry and serve.

—Mary D. Pretlow's
The Calendar of Old Southern Recipes
Courtesy of Kirn Memorial Library

Black Cherry Juice

2 cups wild black cherries
2 tablespoons honey

Place washed cherries in a pan and add just enough water to cover them. Bring to a boil and continue boiling for 15 minutes, mashing them as they cook to extract the juice. Pour through a strainer or cheesecloth to separate from pits. Sweeten with honey and add water to equal 1 quart. Chill and serve.

—Vicki Shufer

Blackberry Wine

To every gallon of berries, put one pint of boiling water. After standing 24 hours, mash the berries well, then squeeze. To every gallon of juice, put 3 pounds of granulated sugar. Put in demijohn to ferment; do not cork until the latter part of November. Keep covered with a net.

—The Old Virginia Cook Book, *1894*

Black Walnuts

Black walnuts are indigenous to the Tidewater area and grow along the edge of cleared farmland and roadsides. The nuts fall from the tree as they ripen in the late fall. When they first drop from the tree, the pods are green and they turn blackish as they dry. When the pods are all black and feel dry, they are ready to be removed by hand or with a paring knife. Underneath the pod is the black walnut still in its shell which must be cracked with a hammer and a great deal of perseverance. But the result is worth it. Your holiday baking will have the distinctive flavor that only black walnuts can give. Princess Anne county natives remember as children preparing for Christmas by cracking the black walnuts with a hammer on a brick.

Black Walnut Cake

Yield: 1 tube cake

1 pound (4 sticks) butter, at
   room temperature
2 cups sugar
9 eggs, separated
1 teaspoon vanilla extract
4 cups sifted flour
½ pound black walnuts,
   floured

Preheat oven to 325 degrees F. Cream butter and sugar. Add egg yolks and vanilla. Add flour gradually, then the beaten egg whites. Beat until well mixed; add nuts. Bake about 1 hour and 15 minutes.

—Edna Grimstead
Table Talk from
Tabernacle United Methodist Church, 1974

Black Walnut Cookies

Yield: about 30

½ cup vegetable shortening
1 cup light brown sugar
1 egg, lightly beaten
1 teaspoon vanilla extract
1½ cups flour
½ teaspoon baking soda
½ teaspoon salt
1 cup chopped black
   walnuts

Frosting
¼ cup maple syrup
4 tablespoons margarine
½ teaspoon maple flavoring
2½ cups confectioner's
   sugar

Preheat oven to 375 degrees F. Cream the shortening and sugar together until light and creamy. Beat in the egg and vanilla. Mix flour, baking soda, and salt and stir into sugar mixture. Stir in black walnuts. Drop by teaspoons onto greased baking sheets and bake 12 to 15 minutes.

To make frosting, heat the syrup. Add butter and stir until it melts. Stir in flavoring and enough sugar to make a spreading consistency. Frost tops of cooled cakes.

—Mary Reid Barrow

Black Walnut Oatmeal Cookies

Yield: 4 dozen

¾ cup granulated sugar
½ cup packed brown sugar
1 cup vegetable shortening
2 eggs, well beaten
1 tablespoon white vinegar
1 teaspoon vanilla extract
2 cups flour
1 teaspoon baking soda
1 teaspoon salt
¼ teaspoon nutmeg
2 cups quick-cooking
  oatmeal
¾ cup raisins
¾ cup chopped black
  walnuts

Preheat oven to 350 degrees F. Cream sugars with shortening; add eggs, vinegar, and vanilla. Sift flour with soda, salt, and nutmeg; blend into creamed mixture. Add oatmeal, raisins, and nuts; mix well. Drop by teaspoonfuls onto greased cookie sheet; flatten with fork dipped in flour. Bake 10 to 12 minutes.

—Shelby Webster

Black Walnut Chocolate Fudge

Yield: about 1½ pounds

3 cups sugar
3 squares chocolate or
  4 tablespoons cocoa
3 tablespoons corn syrup
1 cup evaporated milk
1 teaspoon vanilla extract
½ cup (1 stick) butter or
  margarine
Dash salt
1 cup black walnuts

Stir together first four ingredients and place on medium heat, covered. Cook about 5 minutes until sugar is dissolved. Remove lid and stir. Cook until chocolate dropped in cold water will form a ball. Remove from heat and add vanilla, butter, and salt. Cool about 5 minutes. Beat until it begins to firm up. Add nuts. Pour into greased 8-by-8-inch pan. Cool and cut into squares.

—Effie Munden

Wild Grape Jelly

Wild grapes once were an integral part of the beach flora and still can be found in unspoiled areas. Julia de Witt, who has been making Beach grape jelly for years, lives with her sisters in the first brick, year-round house built in Virginia Beach. The home was built in 1895 on the oceanfront by the first mayor of Virginia Beach, B. P. Holland. Miss de Witt says the best results are obtained by using some grapes that are slightly underripe, when their pectin is highest.

Wild grapes
Sugar

Wash grapes and add to large kettle. Add water to almost the top of the grapes. Boil until soft, between 20 and 30 minutes. Strain the pulp and measure it. Allow 1 cup strained pulp to 1 cup sugar. Boil pulp and sugar for 20 minutes, stirring often and taking care that it does not boil over. Pour into hot jars and seal.

—Julia de Witt

Persimmons

William Strachey said of the persimmon, "... when they are not fully ripe, they are harsh and Choakye, and furr a mann's mouth like Allam, howbeit being taken fully ripe yet is a reasonable pleasant fruict...." Captain John Smith said a green persimmon "will drawe a man's mouth awrie with much torment" but when ripe after the first frost, "is a delicious as an Apricock." The colonists who discovered the persimmon in 1607 quickly learned to harvest the fruit after the first frost when its harsh flavor had turned to sweetness. They took the name from the Powhatan Indians and the fruit became an important part of their fall and winter diet. Persimmon trees still grow wild throughout Virginia Beach. Try them (after the first frost) and you'll be "as pleased as a possom in a 'simmon tree." Wash them, remove the calyx, and process in a food mill for use in baked goods.

Persimmon Bread

Yield: 1 9-by-5-inch loaf

2 cups sifted flour
1 teaspoon baking powder
½ teaspoon salt
1 teaspoon baking soda
1 teaspoon cinnamon
½ teaspoon nutmeg
½ cup vegetable shortening
  or margarine
¾ cup sugar
2 eggs, beaten
1 teaspoon vanilla extract
1 cup persimmon pulp
½ cup nuts

Sift together flour, baking powder, salt, soda, cinnamon, and nutmeg. Cream shortening, sugar, eggs, and vanilla and gradually blend in dry ingredients. Add pulp and nuts. Preheat oven to 375 degrees F. Pour batter and persimmon-nut mixture into a well-greased 9-by-5-by-3-inch loaf pan and let set for 20 minutes before baking. Bake 55 to 60 minutes.

—Ruth Ohlemeyer
from *Audubon Magazine*

Persimmon Chiffon Pie

Yield: 1 9-inch pie

1 cup persimmon pulp
4 egg yolks
⅓ cup sugar
1 envelope unflavored
  gelatin
¼ teaspoon salt
4 egg whites, beaten to soft
  peaks
¼ cup sugar
1 graham cracker pie crust

Beat persimmon and egg yolks together. Mix sugar, gelatin, and salt in saucepan. Stir persimmon and egg yolks into pan. Cook and stir just until mixture comes to boil. Remove from heat. Stir occasionally until mixture mounds on a spoon.

Add sugar to the egg whites and beat to stiff peaks. Stir in the persimmon mix, gently folding it into the beaten egg whites. Pile into a graham cracker crust. Chill.

—Ruth Ohlemeyer
from *Audubon Magazine*

Persimmon Pudding Allen

Yield: 12 servings

2 cups persimmon purée
¾ cup flour
1 tablespoon cinnamon
½ teaspoon baking soda
2 cups white sugar
3 eggs
2 teaspoons vanilla extract
½ cup milk
½ cup (1 stick) melted
    butter or margarine

Preheat oven to 350 degrees F. Purée persimmons through a large strainer with large spoon or potato masher. Sift together dry ingredients and mix at medium speed with purée, milk, eggs, vanilla, and melted butter. Pour into 9-by-13-inch pan and bake for 45 minutes to 1 hour or until firm (knife inserted comes out clean). Chill thoroughly. Cut into squares and serve. Store in refrigerator.

—Margaret Allen

Persimmon Pudding Davis

If persimmons are soft, use your hand to squish them one by one. Shake the pulp into a bowl and then open your hand to discard seeds and skin. If firm, peel them before seeding them. Don't pick persimmons, wait for them to fall.

Yield: 4 servings

1 envelope unflavored
    gelatin
4 tablespoons sugar
½ cup water
1½ cups persimmon pulp
1 cup heavy cream

Mix gelatin and sugar; dissolve in water. Heat until gelatin is completely dissolved. Stir in pulp and refrigerate. Whip cream. Just as mixture starts to set, fold in whipped cream and chill thoroughly.

—Page Davis

Hunter's Paradise

Virginia Beach is on the Atlantic flyway, and ducks and geese always have used the area as a winter stopover. Wildfowl were an important source of food for the early settlers for whom hunting was not a sport but a necessity.

By the late 1800s, however, Back Bay, in the southern part of Virginia Beach, had become a sportsmen's paradise. It was said the wildfowl were so thick in the skies they could be shot down with a cannon.

Northern hunters arriving at Munden Point on the "Sportsmen's Special" train and locals who gunned for a living used other tricks, too, such as live decoys and sink boxes, to shoot as much game as possible. Commercial hunters would haul ducks and geese out of the area in a horse-drawn cart. The birds were piled so high in the carts that they would fall out along the wayside.

Laws preventing commercial gunning, live decoys, and sink boxes were passed in the 1930s, but private gunning clubs remained scattered all over Back Bay.

Hired hands took care of all the dirty work, from picking the birds, to guiding the hunters to the prime spots, to cooking the meals. Hunters were fortified with huge breakfasts of salt mullet and biscuits and later returned to scrumptious dinners of roast duck and goose.

Back Bay Wildlife Refuge was formed in 1938. It was created from the area encompassing the Princess Anne Hunt Club and the Ragged Island Hunt Club. Today most of the other hunt clubs are either torn down or on property owned by the state in False Cape State Park or in the Pocahontas and Trojan Waterfowl Management Area. No hunting is allowed in the wildlife refuge, and hunting in the other areas is strictly controlled by the state.

Sportsmen today may look back in envy at the abundance of game early in the century, but at the same time they must be thankful for the government restrictions and management that enables them to hunt at all.

Canada Geese. Pen and ink by Jan Southard for Back Bay Wildfowl Guild

Bigmouth Bass, Fried or Baked

Fishermen came from across the United States for the bass fishing in Back Bay and Currituck Sound. These bass are delicious fried or baked.

Yield: 4 servings

To Fry
1 4- to 5-pound bass, skinned and filleted
Salt to taste
Cornmeal as needed

Dredge fillets in cornmeal, season, and fry in deep fat until golden brown.

To Bake
1 4- to 5-pound bass, cleaned and scaled
4 strips bacon
1 8-ounce can tomato sauce
8 small potatoes
4 onions, cut in quarters
Salt and pepper to taste

Preheat oven to 375 degrees F. Place fish in pan with a little water. Layer bacon on top. Pour tomato sauce over the fish. Surround fish with onions and potatoes. Salt and pepper all. Cover pan with aluminum foil. Bake at least 1 hour or until flesh is flaky.

—Mary Waterfield

Lazy Man's Duck

Clerk of the Court Curtis Fruit is an avid duck hunter. He says that most of the meat on a wild duck is in its breast. Because of that, he rarely goes to the trouble of picking the ducks he shoots.

"Instead, I simply fillet each side of the breast out," he said. "I mix up some flour, salt, and pepper in a bowl with a top on it and then place the pieces in the bowl and toss them around like you do with Shake and Bake. I then fry the breast halves on a medium setting in about ¼ to ½ inch of oil.

"I like the taste of wild duck and although I've tried baked duck with onions, oranges, apples, etc., and liked it, I much prefer my quicker, simpler way where the flavor is not hidden."

—Curtis Fruit
Clerk of the Circuit Court

How to Roast a Wild Duck

Ducks as desired
Salt and freshly ground
   pepper to taste
Rosemary to taste
Red wine as needed
1 piece bacon per duck

Preheat oven to 425 degrees F. Allow one duck per person for duck lovers. Otherwise one-half duck will do. Sprinkle salt, pepper, and a pinch of rosemary in the cavity of each duck. Place ducks, breast side up, in baking pan. Douse ducks with red wine until bottom of baking pan is covered. Salt and pepper ducks and cover each breast with a strip of bacon. Seal ducks in pan by tightly covering with heavy-duty foil. Bake for 25 to 30 minutes. Uncover and reduce heat to 350 degrees F. for 20 to 30 minutes or until juices run just slightly pink when breast is pricked with fork. Cooking time will vary with the size of the ducks and the number cooked in the pan.

—Gray Dodson

Wild Duck Gumbo

Yield: 2 to 4 servings

2 ducks, dressed
½ cup (1 stick) butter
About 1 cup flour, sifted
1 heaping soup plate
   onions, chopped
1 heaping soup plate celery,
   chopped
3 garlic cloves
1 5-ounce can tomato paste
1 No. 2 can tomatoes,
   peeled
2 teaspoons Accent
1 cayenne pepper, chopped
   fine
1 heaping soup plate green
   bell peppers, chopped
   fine

Boil ducks until tender in slightly salted water to cover. Drain, reserving stock. Melt butter in heavy iron pot and add flour to make dark brown roux of Indian Squaw. Add onions and celery (avoiding celery leaves). Reduce heat and cook until onions and celery brown somewhat. Now add garlic, tomato paste, tomatoes, Accent, cayenne pepper, green peppers, green onions, parsley, oregano, thyme, salt, and black pepper. Add 2 quarts stock from boiled ducks and permit all ingredients to boil rapidly for ½ hour. Meanwhile, cook wild rice according to directions on box. Cut meat from duck carcasses into bite-

1 bunch green onions, tops
   and bottoms, chopped
1 bunch parsley, chopped
   fine, ½ cup reserved
1 coffee spoon oregano
1 coffee spoon thyme
2 tablespoons salt
1 tablespoon black pepper
1 tablespoon gumbo filé
1 box long-grain and wild
   rice

size pieces, discarding bones. Add meat to pot and enough stock to make rich gumbo. Simmer. Add gumbo filé and stir thoroughly. Pour gumbo over wild rice into soup plates. Sprinkle chopped parsley on top. Serve with warm French bread.

—Gray Dodson

North Bay Teal with Potato Gravy

Yield: 2 servings

1 teal, cleaned and cut in
   half
Flour as needed
Salt and pepper to taste
2 to 3 potatoes, diced
1 onion, chopped

Dredge teal in flour and seasonings. Brown quickly on both sides in hot fat. Drain grease off pan. Cover duck with water and simmer 1½ to 2 hours or until tender. For the last half hour add potatoes and onion. Then remove teal to warm platter. Thicken cooking juices with flour and water paste. Add a dash of thyme and pour over duck.

—Mrs. Steve Barnes

Roast Wild Goose

Mary Waterfield, who works at a hunting and fishing club on Knott's Island, says nine out of ten wild geese are tough. Cooking them in water helps to tenderize them, she says.

Yield: 4 to 6 servings

1 goose
Flour as needed
Salt and pepper to taste
1 onion, quartered

Preheat oven to 350 degrees F. Dredge goose in flour and season. Place onion in cavity. Place goose in a roasting pan with 3 cups of water. Cover and cook for about 2½ hours. Uncover and brown for ½ hour at 425 degrees F.

—Mary Waterfield

Mashed Potato Stuffing for Game

Yield: 6 servings

1 small celery stalk with
    leaves, chopped
2 small onions, chopped
½ cup (1 stick) butter or
    margarine, divided
6 servings mashed potatoes
3 teaspoons freshly ground
    black pepper
1½ teaspoons poultry
    seasoning
Salt to taste

Sauté celery and onion in 4 tablespoons butter until onions are translucent. Add to mashed potatoes with pepper, poultry seasoning, salt, and remaining butter. Warm in oven for about 20 minutes while ducks are cooking.

—Gray Dodson

Teeming Waters

"These waters in the winter teem with wild fowl, swan, geese, and ducks of every variety—the canvass-back, mallard, creek, red-head, bald-face, and teal are highly esteemed. The bottom of these waters is covered with a long grass (called wild celery), reaching often to the surface of the water, bearing a number of seed. Some of the ducks feed upon the seed and others upon the roots of this grass. The roots resemble cultivated celery. The delicious flavor of many of these ducks is supposed to be due to this food."

—America. *Homes for Englishmen in the State of Virginia,*
a real estate brochure on Princess Anne County, 1872

Mrs. B. A. Hagood's Quail and Oysters

Salt and pepper to taste
Quail
3 oysters per quail
Melted butter
Cornmeal
Flour
Butter
1 piece bacon per bird

Preheat oven to 400 degrees F. Salt and pepper quail. Wipe birds inside and out with damp cloth. Dip oysters in melted butter, then in cornmeal, and place inside bird. Make flour and butter into a paste and rub breasts well with paste. Place birds in baking dish with strip of bacon across each bird. Bake 30 minutes, basting well with butter. Serve on toast.

—Anne Gilliam

Quail or Dove, Roasted

Dove or quail, dressed
Green pepper
Onion
Melted butter
Fines herbes mixture
Garlic and onion powder

Preheat oven to 325 degrees F. Stuff each dove or quail with a piece of pepper and onion. Pour melted butter over each bird and sprinkle each with fines herbes mixture and garlic and onion powder. Cook, covered tightly, for 30 minutes or until blood just stops running red at joint and meat just begins to pull away from the leg.

—Norvell Butler

"Famous for Its Terrapin"

In 1888 the local newspaper reported the trapping of a huge diamond-back terrapin, eight-and-a-half inches long and weighing five and three-fourths pounds. It was the "largest terrapin ever known in the Norfolk market," the article said. The catch was made at Linkhorn Bay, "famous for its terrapin." "Maryland terrapin alongside ours don't hold contrast because they are so much shorter." it said.

Sautéed Quail

Split dressed quail down the breastbone. Mix commercial tempura batter according to directions or mix a homemade tempura batter. Add a dash of garlic and onion powder to batter. Dip quail in beaten egg and then in batter. Sauté quail in cooking oil until brown.

—Norvell Butler

Marinated Venison

Yield: 8 to 10 servings

4 pounds venison
⅓ cup sherry
⅓ cup soy sauce
⅓ cup vegetable oil
2 tablespoons honey
1 teaspoon ginger
Garlic and onion powder to taste
Bacon as needed

Combine the sherry, soy sauce, oil, honey, ginger, and garlic and onion powders. Marinate the venison all day, turning regularly. Preheat oven to 350 degrees F. Cover the top of the venison with bacon strips in baking pan. Pour sauce around meat and bake covered for 30 to 45 minutes per pound.

—Norvell Butler

Roast Venison

Mary Waterfield works at Barnes' Hunting and Fishing Club on Knotts Island.

Yield: 8 to 10 servings

5- to 8-pound venison roast
1 large onion
½ cup vegetable oil
1 to 1½ cups barbecue sauce

Preheat oven to 350 degrees F. Place venison in roasting pan. Cut up onion on top. Pour oil over top of meat. Cover all with barbecue sauce. Cook 2½ to 3 hours or until tender. Turn oven up to 425 degrees F. and uncover for last ½ hour to brown.

—Mary Waterfield

The Lotus

In the early days of the country, the lotus thrived in the eastern part of the United States. The Indians used it as an important source of food. Sometimes called the water chinquapin, the lotus has tuberous roots which taste like sweet potatoes. Its seeds taste like chestnuts. The Indians even dried the seeds and ground them into a meal and used the young stems and leaves as an herb.

Over the years development along creek beds has caused the lotus to die out, and the last substantial stand in the country is on Tabernacle Creek near Sandbridge, thanks to the efforts of the Cape Henry Women's Club.

In 1955 the club chose the lovely yellow lotus as its club flower, established lotus conservation as one of its primary objectives, and founded the Lotus Festival to call attention to this flower native only to America.

The park area around the lotus gardens has been dedicated to Crezia Reed, the club member who was the driving force behind the festival.

The festival is a week-long event in July during the peak of the lotus-blooming season. The highlight of the week is the luncheon, served, as it has been served for the past thirty years, by the Women of Tabernacle United Methodist Church, which is located across the road from the Lotus Gardens.

Miscellaneous

The Mennonite Presence

All around the Kempsville Borough there are visible signs that the area was and still is, to a degree, a Mennonite colony.

Street names, such as Amish Court and Yoder Lane, two churches, and a school are some of the outward signs of the Mennonite presence. Perhaps the most obvious example of the Mennonite impact on Virginia Beach, however, is Yoder Dairy on Princess Anne Road. The dairy, managed by Mennonites with 50 percent of its employees Mennonites, still will deliver milk in glass bottles with the cream on top to neighborhoods throughout Virginia Beach.

Arriving at the turn of the century, the Mennonites found rural Princess Anne County suited to their simple way of life. They were all dairy, produce, or poultry farmers. Their one indulgence was in the cooking and eating of the fruit of their labors. Mennonites became known for their delicious baked goods, ice cream, and other fine country cooking.

By mid-century, the Mennonites felt the press of urban development and families began emigrating to communities in South Carolina and Georgia where the Norfolk-Virginia Beach Expressway didn't overlook their land.

Mennonites remaining here have adapted externally to ranch-style homes and busy streets. Their faith and their simple, gentle demeanor, however, have not been moved by the trappings of suburbia.

217

Vanilla Ice Cream

Francis Miller manages Yoder Dairy, the last local dairy in Virginia Beach. For more than fifty years Yoder Dairy, a Mennonite business, has been serving Virginia Beach residents with its fresh milk and old-fashioned products such as milk in glass bottles with the cream on top. Jane Miller thinks this vanilla ice cream makes fine use of Yoder Dairy milk and cream.

Yield: 1 gallon

1 quart milk, plus
   3 tablespons, divided
2 cups sugar
½ cup cornstarch
½ teaspoon salt
1 package unflavored
   gelatin
4 eggs, separated, whites
   beaten until stiff
1 quart heavy cream
1 teaspoon vanilla extract

Scald 3 cups milk. Add sugar and stir until blended. Dissolve cornstarch and salt in 1 cup cold milk. Add to hot milk and cook until thick. Beat egg yolks and add slowly to thickened mixture. Cook one more minute. Soak gelatin in 3 table-spoons cold milk and add to hot mixture. Remove custard and cool. Add cream and vanilla. Fold in beaten egg whites. Mix according to directions on ice cream freezer.

—Jane Miller

Almost Healthy Ice Cream Pie

Page Davis worked as the cook at the Tidewater Detention Home and believes good nutrition can have a positive effect on children's behavior.

Yield: 8 servings

Crust
1½ cups whole wheat
   breadcrumbs
2 teaspoons cinnamon
2 tablespoons melted butter
3 tablespoons honey

Combine ingredients and press into springform pan like graham cracker crust.

Filling
4 egg whites
½ cup honey
2 cups heavy cream
1 teaspoon vanilla extract *or*
   ¼ cup any cordial

Whip whites and honey in top of double boiler until stiff.
   Whip the cream and fold in. Add vanilla or cordial. Pour into crust and freeze. Garnish with shaved chocolate.

—Page Davis

Cayce Breakfast Food

American clairvoyant Edgar Cayce, well known for his ability to give accurate health information while in a sleep-like trance, established the Association for Research and Enlightenment in Virginia Beach. People travel to the institution from all over the world to study his readings. Cayce lived in the city from 1925 until his death in 1945. His many suggestions for a healthy, balanced diet featured fresh fruits, vegetables, whole grains, and other natural foods. This recipe was given in several of Cayce's "health readings" as a particularly beneficial food.

Yield: 4 to 5 cups

1 cup black figs, chopped very fine
1 cup dates, chopped very fine
½ cup yellow cornmeal
2 to 3 cups water

Combine dates, figs, cornmeal, and water. Cook over low heat or in double boiler for 15 to 20 minutes. This mixture may be eaten plain or topped with milk, cream, or yogurt for a tasty and healthy breakfast, snack, or dessert.

—Association for Research and Enlightenment

CAYCE HOSPITAL OF RESEARCH AND ENLIGHTENMENT

Early drawing of the Cayce Hospital of Research and Enlightenment which opened in 1928. Courtesy of the Association for Research and Enlightenment Inc.

Brunch Casserole

This is a favorite Sunday morning breakfast of former Virginia Governor John Dalton's family. His wife Eddy says it was often served on summer weekends at Camp Pendleton, the Virgina National Guard base in Virginia Beach, where a vacation retreat for Virginia governors also is located. Eddy Dalton, a fine cook, has two cookbooks to her credit.

Yield: 8 servings

8 slices white bread, crusts trimmed
½ pound sharp cheese, grated
1 pound bulk sausage, cooked but not dry
3 or 4 eggs, depending on size
2 cups milk
½ teaspoon salt
1 teaspoon dry mustard
Dash pepper

Grease a 9-by-13-inch glass dish. Line bottom of dish with bread slices. Sprinkle cheese, then sausage evenly over bread. Mix together eggs, milk, and seasonings and pour over bread, cheese, and sausage mixture. Chill overnight. Preheat oven to 350 degrees F. and bake for 30 to 45 minutes.

—Eddy Dalton

Fried Camembert

Oceana Naval Air Station was established in Virginia Beach in 1941 on 330 acres. In the 1950s, when jet planes were developed, the base was expanded to 5,000 acres and today is is home port for many fighter and attack squadrons. This recipe comes from the Oceana Officers' Wives cookbook, *A Flight Plan Before Dinner,* which is full of wonderful recipes acquired by the wives as they travel around the world with their husbands.

Yield: 2 servings

1 8-ounce round ripe Camembert, with rind
2 tablespoons flour
1 egg, beaten
1 tablespoon milk
1 cup dry breadcrumbs
½ teaspoon salt
4 tablespoons melted butter

Cut cheese in half horizontally, forming two thin rounds; *do not* remove rind. Dredge each round in flour. Combine egg and milk; set aside. Combine breadcrumbs and salt. Dip cheese into egg mixture, and then into breadcrumbs. Cook in butter over medium heat about 1 minute on each side or until brown and crisp.

—Pat Modlin
VF-103, Oceana Naval Air Station
A Flight Plan Before Dinner, 1982

Cheese Wafers

Yield: 5 to 6 dozen wafers

½ pound (2 sticks) butter or margarine, at room temperature
½ pound sharp Cheddar cheese, grated
½ pound flour
½ teaspoon salt
Dash cayenne pepper
Pecans as needed

Cream butter. Add cheese and cream again. Add flour, salt, and pepper, Chill. Make into rolls one inch in diameter. Chill again. Preheat oven to 375 degrees F. Slice thin. Place on ungreased cookie sheet. Place half a pecan on each wafer. Bake for 8 to 10 minutes.

—Mary Reid Barrow

Cheese Strata

This is a favorite dish at the Friends of Music after-concert parties. The Friends was established in 1968 and was the first group to bring classical music concerts to the Beach.

Yield: 8 to 10 servings

4 cups seasoned croutons
8 ounces Cheddar cheese, shredded
1 pound mushrooms, sautéed
1 pound sausage, cooked and crumbled
8 eggs
4 cups milk
1 teaspoon salt
1 teaspoon onion powder
1 teaspoon dry mustard
Pepper to taste

Preheat oven to 325 degrees F. Grease a 3-quart casserole. Layer the croutons, cheese, mushrooms, and sausage in casserole. Beat eggs well and add milk and seasonings. Mix well and pour over layers in casserole. Bake 50 to 60 minutes. Serve with curried fruit and coffee cake.

—Shelby Balderson

Syllabub

This is the kind of elegant drink that might have been served at the Francis Land House in colonial times. Now owned by the city of Virginia Beach, the house on Virginia Beach Boulevard is probably one of the largest of the gambrel-roofed homes built in Princess Anne County and certainly one of the finest. It was built by Francis Land, III in 1732 on land once owned by his grandfather (Francis Land, I), who was one of the largest landowners in the county.
Yield: 8 servings

2 cups heavy cream
¼ cup sugar
1 cup madeira
Juice of 1 lemon
2 egg whites

Chill eight wine glasses. Whip cream and sugar until stiff. Stir in ½ cup madeira with lemon juice. Blend well. Beat egg whites until soft peaks form. Fold into cream mixture. Pour 1 tablespoon madeira into each glass. Spoon cream mixture on top of madeira. Chill and serve.

—Alice McCaw

The Francis Land House, owned by the city of Virginia Beach, was built in 1732 by Francis Land III and is considered one of the more elegant old Princess Anne County residences. Illustration by Alice Walter

Grits Casserole

This casserole is traditionally served at the Good Friday luncheon at Nimmo United Methodist Church. Nimmo Church, built in 1792, is the oldest Methodist Church building standing in Virginia Beach. The only older church in the city is Old Donation Episcopal Church. Located at Oceana Boulevard and Princess Anne Road, the church was restored in 1962. The handsome random-width pine flooring and the slave balcony are two special features. Nimmo was known for its successful revival meetings and the accompanying huge feasts out on the church lawn.

Yield: 8 servings

¾ cup quick-cooking grits
3 cups water
½ pound Cheddar cheese, grated or cubed
½ cup (1 stick) butter
2 eggs, slightly beaten
2 teaspoons seasoned salt
¼ teaspoon cayenne pepper
2 to 3 dashes hot pepper sauce

Preheat oven to 350 degrees F. Bring water to a full boil and add grits. Boil slowly over medium heat until thick, about 3 minutes, stirring frequently. While grits are hot, add remaining ingredients, stirring until well mixed. Pour into well-greased 7-by-11-inch casserole. Bake about 1 hour.
—Gloria Malbon

Mrs. Parks' Egg Alanton

This recipe was served for many years at the annual Christmas breakfast at Alanton Elementary School.

Yield: 12 servings

1 dozen eggs, scrambled very soft
2 cups grated Cheddar cheese
1 large can drained sliced mushrooms
1 can mushroom soup
2 tablespons dry sherry

Preheat oven to 350 degrees F. In large casserole, layer eggs, cheese, and mushrooms. Combine mushroom soup with sherry and pour over egg mixture. Bake for 45 minutes. This can be prepared the day before and baked just before serving.
—Caroline Kennett

George Washington's Egg Nog

Yield: almost a gallon

1 dozen eggs
12 tablespoons sugar
1 pint brandy
½ pint rye
¼ pint Jamaica rum
¼ pint sherry
1 quart milk
1 quart cream

Beat eggs, gradually adding sugar. Slowly add liquors. Then add milk and cream, still stirring. Let mellow a day or two in the refrigerator.

—Mary Reid Barrow

Carob

For ten years, Famarco Limited in Virginia Beach has been producing Martin's Virginia Roast Carob Powder which is shipped around the nation. Carob powder can be used in place of cocoa measure-for-measure. Three tablespoons of powder will replace a one-ounce square of baking chocolate. Carob is a favorite with health food aficionados, because it is caffeine-free, has 40 percent fewer calories, and 85 percent less sodium than cocoa. Also, carob's natural sugar content is 46 percent while cocoa contains only about 5½ percent natural sugar.

Carob Nut Slices

Yield: 20 slices

½ cup chunk-style peanut
  butter
¼ cup raisins
2 tablespoons Martin's
  Carob Powder
2 tablespoons honey
4 teaspoons non-fat dry
  milk
1 tablespoon sesame seeds,
  toasted in skillet over
  moderate heat

In a small bowl combine peanut butter, raisins, carob powder, honey, and dry milk until mixture is well blended. Roll mixture on waxed paper into a 10-inch log. Roll in sesame seeds. Wrap and chill for at least 2 hours. Cut log into ½-inch thick slices; serve cold.

—Famarco Limited

Carob Honey Cake

Yield: 1 9-inch cake

1 cup pastry flour
½ cup Martin's Carob
  Powder
1½ teaspoons cinnamon
6 egg yolks
⅓ cup butter, at room
  temperature
½ cup honey
⅓ cup water
2 teaspoons vanilla extract
6 egg whites, stiffly beaten

Frosting
4 tablespoons honey
3 tablespoons butter, at
  room temperature
⅔ cup milk powder
⅓ cup Martin's Carob
  Powder, sifted
4 tablespoons light cream
½ teaspoon vanilla extract
½ cup nuts, finely chopped

Preheat oven to 350 degrees F. Combine flour, carob, and cinnamon. Mix well. Beat egg yolks with butter and honey. Add water and vanilla. Combine dry and wet mixtures and mix thoroughly, and then fold in beaten egg whites.

Grease a 9-inch springform pan with butter, pour in batter, and bake for about 45 minutes. Cool, then ice with frosting.

To make frosting: in a medium-size mixing bowl, cream honey and butter. Stir in milk powder and carob. Add cream and vanilla. Beat until smooth. Stir in nuts and spread over cake.

—Famarco Limited

Chocolate Fudge

Yield: about 2 pounds

½ cup (1 stick) butter
4½ cups sugar
1 large can evaporated milk
3 small packages chocolate chips
1 8-ounce jar marshmallow cream
1 cup nuts
1 teaspoon vanilla extract

Cook butter, sugar, and milk for 7 minutes. Add chocolate chips, marshmallow cream, nuts, and vanilla. Pour onto greased cookie sheet.

—Mary Cooper

Cavalier Supreme Pie

This is a "secret" recipe which was given to Jane Tucker by the chef at the old Cavalier Hotel when she owned a gift shop there more than twenty years ago.

Yield: 1 8-inch pie

1 tablespoon unflavored gelatin
½ cup cold water
½ cup hot milk
5 tablespoons confectioner's sugar, divided
3 egg yolks
½ cup milk
Pinch salt
1 8-inch pie crust, baked
½ pint heavy cream, whipped
1 tablespoon rum
Shaved bitter or semi-sweet chocolate

Soften gelatin in cold water. Dissolve with hot milk. Beat 5 tablespoons of sugar, egg yolks, and milk. Add to gelatin mixture. Add salt. Allow to cool a bit and pour into pie crust. Make a meringue of the whipping cream, 2 tablespoons sugar, and rum. Cover pie with cream and refrigerate 3 hours or more before serving. Garnish with shaved chocolate.

—Jane Tucker

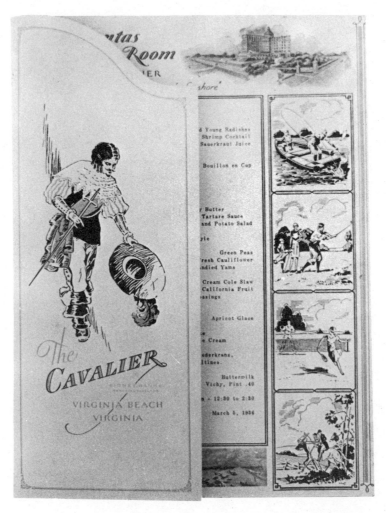

Cavalier Hotel Menu, circa 1930. Courtesy of Kirn Memorial Library

Mary Nash Herbert Hoggard's Wine Jelly

This is Alice Walter's grandmother's recipe. For a modern touch, Mrs. Walter often substitutes a large package of lemon-flavored gelatin for the sugar, plain gelatin, and lemon juice.

Yield: 4 servings

1 quart water
Peel and juice of 1 lemon
1 cup of raisins
2 to 3 sticks cinnamon
2 to 3 sprigs mace
2 packages unflavored
   gelatin
¾ to 1 cup sugar
2 cups sherry

Combine ingredients and bring to a boil; then simmer until reduced by half the water, lemon peel, raisins, cinnamon, and mace. Soften gelatin with juice of lemon. Strain hot spiced water and pour over gelatin. Add sugar. Stir until sugar and gelatin are dissolved. Add two cups sherry.

—Alice Walter

Pulled Candy

One of the highlights of a family get-together in the country was a candy pulling. This recipe belonged to Mary Knight Malbon. She was such a good cook that her son compiled her recipes into a Malbon family cookbook!

Yield: about 1 pound

2 cups sugar
¼ cup vinegar
¼ cup water
½ cup chopped nuts

Boil ingredients in a pan until the mixture spins a thread when dropped from a spoon, or boil until hard boil stage on candy thermometer. Pour into a greased flat container until candy cools enough to handle. Grease hands well with butter and pull until candy turns white or starts to harden. Shape into a long roll and cut in inch-size pieces.

—Margery Malbon Theberge

Chocolate Meringue Pie

This is an old family recipe which belonged to Mrs. Kellam's mother.

Yield: 1 9-inch pie

3 cups milk
2 squares chocolate
1 cup sugar
2 eggs, separated
2 heaping tablespoons
   cornstarch
Water as needed
1 teaspoon vanilla extract
1 tablespoon butter
1 9-inch pie shell, baked
2 tablespoons sugar
Pinch salt
Pinch cream of tartar

Place milk, chocolate, and sugar in top of double boiler and cook until hot, stirring occasionally to melt chocolate. Mix egg yolks and cornstarch with enough water to make a thin paste and add to hot mixture. Stir until it comes to a boil and is smooth. Remove from heat and add vanilla and butter. Pour into pie shell. Preheat oven to 350 degrees F. Place egg whites in medium mixing bowl and beat at high speed with electric mixer. Sprinkle sugar, salt, and cream of tartar on whites without stopping beater. Beat until stiff. Spread on pie. Bake until meringue is lightly browned.

—Odie Kellam

Elegant Farmer Grasshopper Pie

Yield: 1 9-inch pie

24 Oreo cookies, finely
   crushed
4 tablespooons melted
   butter
¼ cup creme de menthe
1 pint jar marshmallow
   cream
2 cups heavy cream,
   whipped

Combine cookies and butter; press into 9-inch springform pan, saving ½ cup for topping. Blend creme de menthe and marshmallow; fold in whipped cream. Pour into crust. Freeze until firm.

—Page Davis

Snow Pudding

This has been Elizabeth Atwood's favorite dessert for many years. She is a descendant of the Nimmos for whom Nimmo United Methodist Church is named.

Yield: 4 servings

1 package unflavored
  gelatin
¼ cup cold water
1 cup boiling water
¾ cup sugar
¼ cup lemon juice
Grated peel of 1 lemon
Whites of 2 eggs
Salt to taste

Boiled Custard
2 cups milk
2 egg yolks, beaten
½ cup sugar
1 tablespoon flour
1 teaspoon vanilla extract

Soften gelatin in cold water. Dissolve in boiling water. Add sugar, lemon juice, and peel, stirring until sugar is dissolved also. Let mixture begin to jell. Beat egg whites and salt until stiff and fold into gelatin mixture. Refrigerate until firm. Serve with boiled custard.

To make custard: Heat milk in saucepan. Combine sugar and flour. Gradually add sugar and flour to egg yolks, beating. Add ½ cup hot milk slowly to yolk mixture, stirring constantly. Return milk and yolks to saucepan, slowly, stirring constantly, and simmer, stirring, until mixture coats the back of a spoon. Remove from stove. Add vanilla. Chill.

—Elizabeth Atwood

Real Butter Mints

Yield: 1¼ pounds mints

4 tablespoons butter
1 pound confectioner's
  sugar
8 drops oil of peppermint
2 tablespoons cold water

Mix all ingredients in food processor; or melt butter, stir in sugar, oil of peppermint, and water. Knead until smooth and firm. Form into balls. Make a crisscross pattern on top with fork, or form in a mint mold.

—Page Davis